How to Write Winning Short Stories

A Companion Workbook

Nancy Sakaduski

©2020 Nancy Sakaduski
All rights reserved. Published 2020.
ISBN: 978-1-7323842-6-2
Printed in the United States of America

No part of this publication may be reproduced or transmitted in any form or by any means, electronic or mechanical, including photocopy, recording, or any information storage and retrieval system, without permission in writing from the publisher.

Special thanks to Nancy Powichroski Sherman and Robin Hill-Page Glanden for their thoughtful input and guidance.

Cat & Mouse Press
Lewes, DE 19958
www.catandmousepress.com

Contents

Getting Started	3
Details	27
Illustration vs. Explanation	35
The Ending	43
Premise and Theme	49
Structure	55
Pacing	63
Setting	69
Characters	77
Point of View	87
Dialogue	97
The Title	105
Editing	111
Facts, Logic, and Lawyers	123
Marketing Short Stories	129
Putting It All Together	139
Answer Key	147

Introduction

How to Use This Workbook

This workbook is based on the book *How to Write Winning Short Stories*. It is designed for people who want to immediately convert knowledge to action. While this workbook contains some bare bones information from the book, the workbook is intended to supplement—not replace— *How to Write Winning Short Stories*.

How to Write Winning Short Stories is a practical manual that provides accessible, actionable advice to short story writers, particularly beginning or emerging writers, who want to write short stories for adult readers. The *How to Write Winning Stories Workbook* should serve as a writing coach, encouraging you to apply what you have learned and, through practical exercises, see how these skills can be used in your own writing.

This workbook follows the order of the content in the book but focuses on topics that lend themselves to exercises and practice. Take your time going through each section, repeating the exercises you find difficult and revisiting the book for additional insights as you work on your own story or novel.

Good things, when short, are twice as good.

-Baltasar Gracián

Chapter 1

GETTING STARTED

Short stories are fun and challenging to write. They contain many of the components of a novel (setting, characters, plot), but those elements must be realized in a short format that forces discipline and economy. Short stories provide a place to showcase smaller ideas and less complex plots. They allow the writer to create more drama in a shorter span of time.

With a short story, the writer must telegraph information. There is no room for long explanations, large casts of characters, or sweeping expanses of time. Backstory is kept to a minimum—only what is needed to understand the character's actions—and although the ending should be satisfying, it doesn't have to explain everything.

Short stories are distinguished by their focus and intensity. It is even more important to use active voice, specific verbs, and descriptive nouns. Each word should be chosen carefully, and each sentence well constructed. The writer must grab the reader's attention immediately and have that reader experiencing the story as quickly as possible. And because short stories are usually read in one sitting, readers are more likely to remember the beginning and all that has transpired when they reach the ending.

Story Length

The length of a short story can range from extremely short (under one hundred words) to near novella length (ten thousand words). A length of seventy-five hundred or eight thousand is often used as an upper guide, with one thousand to five thousand words being the most common length. Anything below one thousand starts to get into the realm of flash fiction or even micro fiction (under one hundred words).

What length should your story be? It depends on both the story and your writing style. If your story is more plot than character, perhaps featuring a twist or punchline ending, it may be well suited to flash fiction. If you have multiple characters, a complex plot, or changes in time (flash forwards or flashbacks), it may be better written as a longer story. If your style is to build tension slowly and fill your scenes with poetic description or character introspection, you may become frustrated with extremely short forms.

Although there is nothing wrong with writing for your own pleasure, writing for publication requires matching the work to the outlet. Take the time to identify potential outlets before you begin writing. Selecting one or more potential submission opportunities will also give you some parameters (maximum word count, for example) that will add structure to your project.

Genre

Short stories may or may not fall into a genre (science fiction, romance, mystery, fantasy). If you plan to write a genre short story, be sure to read books and stories in that genre to learn its language and conventions.

The genre you choose should be appropriate for your story and your writing style. If your writing tends to have a lot of action, swift transitions, and snappy dialogue, you may want to try a thriller, science fiction, or fantasy. If your writing tends to focus on relationships and introspection, you may want to try romance or even memoir.

When you're planning your story, you can start anywhere you want. You may have the characters in mind first and then need to come up with challenges to throw their way. Or you may have created a perfect climax for a story and now need to set up plot points that lead to it.

Sometimes the genre will guide the planning process. If you want to write a mystery story, for example, the plot may revolve around a murder, and that will guide much of the planning. With a short story you don't have the space for multiple major events unless they tie together in theme and lead to a climax.

One excellent source for ideas is your own inner fears or dreams. Think about emotional triggers—a time you hit someone (or were hit), a grand plan that went up in smoke, the first time you said "I love you," a moment of defeat, a time you feared for your life, something you did that made you ashamed. What makes you cry? What makes you angry?

You can use real life as a starting point, but don't let the truth get in the way of a good story. Examine events from your life and remember a feeling you had (guilt, humiliation, joy, anger), and then consider what might have happened if you'd made a different choice.

The traditional advice of "write what you know" has value because when the author has firsthand knowledge, the writing tends to be more detailed and vivid than that derived completely from research or the imagination. Look for ways your expertise can add authenticity. Don't bury readers with a deluge of explanation, but a few authentic details can add spark to a story. This can be in the form of inside knowledge, specialized terms, or character details.

After nourishment, shelter and companionship, stories are the thing we need most in the world.

-Philip Pullman

Worksheet — Exercise: 1-1

Characteristics of Short Stories: True or False?

___ In short stories, the writer must telegraph information rather than provide lengthy explanations.

___ Short stories usually provide complete backstories that explain how the characters came to be who they are.

___ Short stories have less drama and impact than novels.

___ Readers are usually willing to give short stories more time to get started.

___ Short stories usually have fewer characters.

___ The ending of a short story should tie up all the loose ends.

___ Complicated ideas and complex plots lend themselves better to novels than short stories.

___ Short stories often cover a longer span of time.

___ In short stories, there is even less room for unnecessary detail and for nouns and verbs padded with adjectives and adverbs.

___ Short stories are essentially the same as novels; they're just shorter.

Worksheet — Exercise: 1-2

Choosing What to Write

What Should You Write? Check any of the following that apply:

- __ I use a lot of imagery and poetic language in my writing.
- __ I like surprise endings.
- __ I love to analyze relationships and tend to use a lot of dialogue.
- __ My background is journalism or nonfiction writing.
- __ I have a short attention span and get eager to move on to the next project.
- __ My characters tend to be complex and have rich emotional lives.
- __ I have lots of ideas for stories.
- __ I like to have a theme that is woven into the story.
- __ My stories tend to have only one or two characters.
- __ I love using flashbacks to fill in backstory.
- __ My stories tend to have multiple settings.
- __ I like to get right to the point.
- __ I like to tell stories from multiple points of view.
- __ I love world building (creating a fictional universe with its own societies and rules).
- __ I like family sagas that show multiple generations of the same family.
- __ I like to work quickly and get the job done.
- __ My writing tends to be concise (not filled with description, narration, complex relationships).
- __ I love planning, outlining, mapping, and other organizational activities.
- __ I like to share in-depth information about my occupation, hobby, or special interest through my characters.

Worksheet   Exercise: 1-3

Should You Write Short Stories?

Check the statements that apply to you:

___ I like to experiment with my writing.

___ I love the research part of writing.

___ I would rather work on many short projects than commit to one long project.

___ I have lots of ideas.

___ I like stories that are told in real time or over a short span of time.

___ I like to write stories with complex themes and multiple story lines.

___ I have more energy than patience.

___ I have a short attention span and get eager to move on to the next project.

___ My stories tend to have large casts of characters.

___ I like to get right into the action.

___ I have little uninterrupted writing time.

___ I can't decide what to write because there are so many things I'd like to write about.

___ I have developed a character or group of characters I really like.

___ I'm not sure what kind of writing I want to do (mysteries, thrillers, romance, etc.).

___ I like to pit one character against another.

Idea Grid

Starting Point	Where to Use	Impact	Possible Twists	Research Needed	Setting Options
Inner Fear					
Dream					
Memory					
Discovery					
My Expertise					
My Experience					
Motivates Me					
Emotional Trigger					
Person I Know					
Place I've Been					
Something Funny					
Common Problem					
Conflict					
Deadly Sin					

Submission Notes

Potential Outlets: Submission Grid

Outlet	Type of Pub	Genre Need	Words	Audience	Requirements	Deadline

Evaluate Your Writing

Getting Started Checklist

☐ I considered the potential market for my story.

☐ If I chose a genre (mystery, romance, fantasy), I read many stories and researched the genre's characteristics.

☐ I have a writing space that suits my needs.

☐ I decided on the type of story I want to write.

☐ I read high-quality short stories for education and inspiration.

☐ I mined my own experiences for ideas.

☐ I have an idea file for collecting photos, articles, and notes for future stories.

☐ I developed at least a basic synopsis for my story.

☐ My own experiences will help me, but I'm not letting real life stand in the way of a great story.

Chapter 2

THE IMPORTANCE OF STORY

The first few sentences of your story determine whether someone continues to read. Do readers find the story compelling? Do they care about the character(s)? Does the story's time and place interest them? Is it worth their time to read?

One of the best ways to hook the reader is to open in the middle of the action, which provides excitement and curiosity. How did this happen? What's going on here? You might open in the middle of a conversation that provides insights into the characters, reveals something about the setting, and hints at the conflict. You might open with the setting in a way that creates fear, curiosity, or other emotions. You might open with a question, and then move to another scene, leaving the question unanswered for the moment. Just make sure that you ground the reader quickly and provide clues to the location, so the characters don't seem to be floating around in space.

One approach to creating a captivating beginning is to simply write the story and then go back and think about where the best place would be to *open* the story. It may not be where you started; it may be a few paragraphs or even pages into your initial telling.

Never start with backstory. Start with a conflict or threat, something unusual or unexpected, an intriguing conversation, or just about anything that will make the reader want to find out more. Put characters (especially the main character) in motion quickly. Grab and emotionally hook the reader immediately.

Deciding where to start a story is one of the most important decisions you will make. Remember that the beginning is not what happens before the story starts, it's what happens *when* the story starts.

> *Tell the readers a story! Because without a story, you are merely using words to prove you can string them together in logical sentences.*
>
> -Anne McCaffrey

Worksheet — Exercise: 2-1

The Importance of Story True/False

___ One of the best ways to hook a reader is to start the story by describing the main character's background.

___ It's possible to convey some of a character's backstory through action.

___ The first few sentences of a story often determine whether a reader continues to read.

___ You should never open a story with a question.

___ It's important to ground the reader quickly by providing clues to the location.

___ The best place to start a story may not be where you started writing it.

___ Deciding where to start a story is one of the most important decisions the writer makes.

___ It's important to describe the main character right away.

___ One way to convey backstory is with unspoken thoughts.

___ It's important to put characters in motion quickly.

___ If you open the story with a question, be sure you answer it before moving on.

___ It's OK to just write the story from the beginning, but when you're finished you should go back and make sure that's the best place to open the story.

___ You should never start a story with dialogue.

___ A mystery story should always start with the murder.

Worksheet

Exercise: **2-2**

Choosing the Story Opener

Circle the ways to start a story that are most likely to engage the reader:

1. Dialogue between two men planning a crime

2. Information about a historical event that is key to the story

3. A scene featuring a skydiver jumping out of a plane

4. A character describing his hobby

5. The recounting of an event that took place in an earlier time

6. An exclamation such as "You've got to be kidding me!"

7. Description of an operating room door closing

8. Unspoken dialogue such as: *And yet again, I find myself saying yes.*

9. Explanation of the relationship between the two main characters

10. A scene that shows a robot being constructed

11. Two characters having breakfast and discussing the day ahead

12. Description of the main character's appearance

13. Someone slapping another person's face

14. A question such as "What do you want?"

15. Explanation of how something works that is important in the story

16. A child being kidnapped

17. A woman making beef stew

18. An odd contrast such as a crow in a church or a clown asking a police officer for directions

19. Description of a Little League game

Worksheet

Exercise: 2-3

Knowing Where to Start

Read the beginning of this story and determine where you would choose to start it.

It was a warm day in September. Claire pushed her long blond hair off her face as she closed the door to her tidy Nantucket bungalow. She had lived on the island for six years, working as a copy editor for the local paper. As she got to her car, she noticed that the tires were flat.

Again. Claire gazed up the quiet Nantucket street. Her tires had been slashed for the second time in little more than a week. *This has got to stop.*

Claire strode into the press room of the *Nantucket Gazette*, dropped her handbag and laptop at her workstation, and wheeled around the corner to confront Silas.

"You're not going to get away with this." Claire glared at Silas, who gazed up from his computer with an annoyed expression.

"What's that then?"

"You know what. My tires are slashed. This has got to stop."

Silas smirked. "It will stop when you stop slashing my copy."

Worksheet

Exercise: **2-4**

Converting Backstory 1

Using action, with or without dialogue or unspoken thoughts, bring some or all of this backstory to life:

Dorothy is eighty-five and matriarch of the family. She lives alone in the family home, a large farmhouse in rural Pennsylvania. Her sons, Don and Ed, want her to move into assisted living, but as someone who has always been in charge, she can't bear the thought. Her daughter, Lisa, has just arrived for a visit. Lisa's brothers want her to convince their mother to move but Lisa hates confrontations. She has problems of her own and feels she has never measured up to her mother's expectations.

Worksheet

Exercise: **2-5**

Converting Backstory 2

Using action, with or without dialogue or unspoken thoughts, bring some or all of this backstory to life:

> Sherry is an only child and her parents had high expectations for her. She is thirty-five and has been living with Mike for five years. He has had trouble keeping a job (he'd rather party), so she works as a waitress instead of finishing her degree. They recently bought a mobile home in Salisbury. Her parents are about to arrive for a visit. They wanted to surprise her, so the only warning she had was a call from the airport.

_____

_____

_____

_____

_____

_____

_____

_____

_____

_____

_____

_____

Worksheet

Exercise: **2-6**

Converting Backstory 3

Using action, with or without dialogue or unspoken thoughts, bring some or all of this backstory to life:

> Katie has moved to California in hopes of breaking into TV or film. She has the looks but not the connections. Years of dance, singing, and modeling lessons have prepared her for this moment. An inheritance has funded the move and provided money to cover about six months of living expenses. She feels a bit guilty, as she knows her brother really needs the money, but this is her big chance.

_____
_____
_____
_____
_____
_____
_____
_____
_____
_____
_____

Evaluate Your Writing

The Importance of Story Checklist

- ❑ I have a story (characters, conflict, action, and resolution).

- ❑ I grounded the reader quickly, without getting bogged down with backstory.

- ❑ I started the story in the right place.

- ❑ I looked for ways to use action and dialogue or unspoken thoughts to convey backstory.

- ❑ I put the characters into motion quickly.

- ❑ I provided backstory along the way and in small doses instead of an info dump.

- ❑ My story opens with a strong hook.

Chapter 3

CONFLICT

A winning story relies on a central conflict—a problem for the character to solve, overcome, or be consumed by. The problem provides a reason for the reader to care, catches the reader's interest, and creates curiosity. Conflict propels the character to action. In a short story, the problem cannot be so big that it can't be resolved, or at least mitigated, in a satisfactory way within the space of a short story.

Create the problem, then raise the stakes. Introduce an obstacle that prevents the character from achieving the goal. The conflict can be internal or external, can be between characters or within a character, or can involve an external force. Obstacles can be another character (antagonist), time, space, a personality flaw, or another factor that stands between the character and the goal. The obstacles could be unintended consequences of decisions the character makes, which force another choice and may lead to additional problems. Each failure should have consequences to build tension but should be a small step toward the solution.

Want to bump up the tension? Put a clock on it. Create a deadline that must be met, whether it's a race to defuse a bomb or an all-or-nothing romantic rendezvous. The tension in the story should lead to a pivotal scene—the climax of the story. The climax should not be rushed, as much of the reader's enjoyment of the story depends on how well the key incident of the story is told.

Good fiction's job is to comfort the disturbed and disturb the comfortable. -David Foster Wallace

Worksheet

Exercise: **3-1**

Conflict True/False

__ A central conflict is an important part of a story.

__ The central conflict can be something for the character to solve, overcome, or be consumed by.

__ To increase conflict, lower the stakes.

__ A time limit can increase tension.

__ A personality flaw can serve as an obstacle for a character to overcome.

__ Conflict propels a character into action.

__ The pivotal scene (climax) of the story should be quick so the character can move on.

__ A character's decisions and failures should have consequences.

__ Conflict must come from the outside (be external).

__ A moral dilemma is one type of conflict.

Worksheet

Exercise: **3-2**

Identify Conflict in a Story

The Wizard of Oz

_____

_____

Romeo and Juliet

_____

_____

Star Wars

_____

_____

Gone with the Wind

_____

_____

The King's Speech

_____

_____

The Hunger Games

_____

_____

The Perfect Storm

_____

_____

Apollo 13

_____

_____

Pride and Prejudice

_____

_____

Worksheet

Exercise: **3-3**

Create Conflict

It's more challenging to create conflict within the confines of a short story, but it can certainly be done. Consider the following description of a scene and suggest some possible sources of conflict and ways to convey it in a short story.

A couple is sitting at the breakfast table. The man is reading the newspaper and the woman is going over her day's schedule on her phone. They have two children. One is away at college; the other is upstairs, getting dressed for school.

Conflict Chart

Conflict	Characters Affected	Stakes/Time Limit	Actions Taken	Obstacles/ Complications	Actions Taken	Results

Evaluate Your Writing

Conflict Checklist

- ❑ My story has a central conflict.

- ❑ The conflict is a good match with the theme, genre, and tone of the story.

- ❑ I created one or more obstacles for the main character.

- ❑ The character has taken actions to overcome the obstacles.

- ❑ The character's actions have had consequences.

- ❑ I found ways to raise the stakes.

- ❑ The main character's actions have affected other characters and carried the story forward.

- ❑ Each failure has consequences that build tension and lead toward the solution.

- ❑ I took care to ensure that the climax of the story is not rushed.

- ❑ The central conflict is resolved or mitigated in a satisfying way.

Chapter 4

DETAILS

As you write your story, include specific, telling details about the setting, characters, emotions, and situations. Details bring a story to life and help readers set their mind stage for the events. The best details go another step and reveal character, illuminate emotion, and help drive the story.

> *"The Telling Detail is a word, phrase, or image that helps the reader 'see' what you're describing. It must be precise and illuminating, and to some extent, unique. Its uniqueness is often what makes it so telling."* - Rachelle Gardner

When selecting details, go beyond just the visual. Choose offbeat, less common but more informative, sensory details and include smells, tastes, textures, and sounds.

Look for slang and specialized, regional, or even foreign terms your readers may not be familiar with to add atmosphere and authenticity to your story. If you use the words in a context where your readers will be able to figure out their meaning, it will make the readers feel clever and teach them something along the way.

When doing your research, look for terms that enrich the story. Check all specific details to verify they are accurate, and make sure that any details you mention when writing from a character's viewpoint are details that character would be likely to have noticed and recognized.

The words a character chooses are also telling. A farmer observing the weather would use different words than a sailor, a storm chaser, an event planner, or a meteorologist. Technical terms used by technical people provide depth and legitimacy.

When describing characters, make the description do double duty. Description should allow the reader to form a visual but should also tell us about the character's personality and background. Descriptions given through the eyes of another character filter the perception with attitudes, prejudices, and background. Don't limit your details to adjectives. You can show detail in many ways. Instead of writing that someone had a loud sneeze, you could describe a startled bystander or have a character question whether her sneezes are the reason the pictures on the wall are crooked.

Consider withholding a key piece of information, a relationship between two characters, a past event, or other information that will have the reader wondering for a while. A little misdirection (keep it fair) can confound your character and delay satisfaction.

> *Description begins in the writer's imagination but should finish in the reader's.*
>
> -Stephen King

Worksheet

Exercise: 4-1

Details True/False

__ Details can reveal emotions.

__ A telling detail must be verbal (in dialogue).

__ Telling details are precise and illuminating.

__ The best details are visual.

__ Slang, regionalisms, and foreign terms should be avoided.

__ Details mentioned by a character should be in keeping with the character's age and background.

__ The best details are adjectives.

__ Details should be included in description rather than in dialogue or action.

__ Research can help identify details to include in the story.

__ A writer should avoid withholding information from the reader.

__ Telling details are more specific than general details.

__ Details can convey inner character as well as physical appearance.

__ The details a character chooses to mention can be revealing.

__ Telling details must be technical or more complex.

__ When choosing details, try to include different senses (sounds, smells, textures, etc.).

Worksheet

Exercise: 4-2

Adding Details

Identify places where details could help bring characters and setting to life in this edited excerpt from* The Sea Sprite Inn *by Lynnette Adair:

> Jillian went to her grandfather's home. She could hardly believe it had been so long since she had last been here. Standing in the front yard, she noticed how run-down the house was. The columns were weather-beaten. Above them were a broken window and trim that was missing pieces. Her friend had warned her Gramps' place was looking rough, but it was worse than she expected. Jillian had suffered, too. Moving back into her childhood home had seemed like a good solution, especially since Gramps would need help when he got home.

_____

_____

_____

_____

_____

_____

_____

_____

_____

_____

_____

_____

_____

_____

_____

_____

Worksheet

Exercise: **4-3**

Spot Mistakes with Details

Explain what is wrong with each of the following:

Paul had brown hair parted on the side, blue eyes, and was of medium height.

On Emma's way to elementary school that morning, she noticed that the kousa dogwood trees had started to bloom.

World War II was coming to a close and the soldiers were happy to spend their free Saturday nights watching *The Ed Sullivan Show*.

Miranda bent down and picked up the *gumiszalag*.

Peggy ate another veggie chip and smiled at her Mommy. "I like these whatever-they-ares."

The room had blue walls, two windows, a door to the kitchen, and a rug on the floor.

"This looks like a Migration Period sword, which was popular during the Merovingian period. It was derived from the Roman-era spatha and gave rise to the Carolingian sword of the eighth to eleventh centuries."

She pulled up in front of the very large house.

"Hand me that Johnson screwdriver," said Meg.

Worksheet
Exercise: 4-4

Creating Telling Details

Telling details are illuminating and provide insights beyond just being specific. Fill in the chart below.

General	Detail	Specific Detail	Telling Detail
Place to spend the night			
Place to eat			
Transportation			
Clothing			
Pet			

Evaluate Your Writing

Details Checklist

- ❏ I chose specific, telling details.

- ❏ I used sensory details that go beyond just visual.

- ❏ My characters mention details they would plausibly notice and understand.

- ❏ I used details to illuminate characters' emotions, personality, and background.

- ❏ My details are conveyed in actions and dialogue, as well as in description.

- ❏ I looked for opportunities to withhold information to add interest.

- ❏ I replaced general details with more specific and illuminating ones.

- ❏ I looked for opportunities to include technical terms, foreign words, regionalisms, or slang.

- ❏ If I used unusual terms, I used them in a context that allows readers to figure out their meaning.

- ❏ For any characters with specialized skills or technical occupations, I included details that the characters are likely to know.

- ❏ My character descriptions are more than just physical characteristics such as hair color and height.

Chapter 5

ILLUSTRATION VS. EXPLANATION

Look for ways to illustrate rather than narrate (that's another way of saying "show, don't tell"). People like to experience things, not just be told about them. Rather than write, "It was a dark and stormy night," let the reader hear thunder, feel the rain, and struggle to get the umbrella up.

Check your writing for places where you described emotions, character attributes (especially personality), or setting that could be illustrated instead. If you find yourself writing something involving emotions (James was angry), look for ways to show this through action (James threw the car keys at Sarah) or dialogue ("Get out," James shouted.). Character traits such moodiness, thrift, kindness, impatience, disorganization, and the like can be conveyed through action (He scooped up the fast food containers, mail, and other debris from the passenger seat and tossed them into the back to make room.). Setting, especially weather, can be described through actions (putting on gloves, wiping sweat) or dialogue ("You're so lucky to have a view of the mountains.").

One indication that you have not conveyed sensations or emotions directly is the use of filter words. Filter words such as saw, felt, and heard create distance between the sensation and the reader. Instead of saying "Sheila felt cold," say "Sheila shivered" or show Sheila putting on a coat.

Resist the urge to explain and make sure you're not telling readers things you've already shown through dialogue and action. Dialogue and action, when carefully constructed, can carry a lot of narrative weight as long as you don't try to pile on too much too fast. Look for ways to get your readers into the story and let them experience it for themselves.

> *Don't tell me the moon is shining; show me the glint of light on broken glass.*
>
> -Anton Chekhov

Worksheet
Exercise: 5-1

Illustration vs. Explanation True/False

__ Narration is the best way to tell a story.

__ To bring characters to life, the writer should describe their emotions.

__ Setting can be described through actions.

__ The clearest way to describe an emotion is just to state it: James was angry.

__ Character traits such as kindness can be conveyed through action or dialogue.

__ "Show, don't tell" means to use description rather than dialogue or actions to convey setting or character.

__ Weather is the only part of setting that can't be described through actions.

__ Instead of stating that a character heard something, the author might include a sound effect or character reaction.

__ Using action and dialogue to convey situations helps provide a richer experience for the reader.

__ Personality must be described; it can't be portrayed through actions.

__ To make sure readers understand, the writer should reinforce dialogue or actions through explanation.

__ "Felt" is one of the filter words that separate readers from the character's experience.

Worksheet

Exercise: 5-2

Show, Don't Tell

Convert these sentences into ones that show rather than tell:

1. Hazel was old.

_____

_____

2. Bob was embarrassed.

_____

_____

3. The house was big.

_____

_____

4. It was a hot day.

_____

_____

5. Barbara was tired of Phil's lies.

_____

_____

6. Luke was a cheapskate.

_____

_____

Worksheet

Exercise: **5-2**

Show, Don't Tell, continued

7. She saw the car coming toward her.

_____

_____

8. He heard a whizzing sound as the bullet passed him.

_____

_____

9. The cottage was near the ocean.

_____

_____

Worksheet

Exercise: **5-3**

Show or Tell?

Using an S or T, indicate whether the following show or tell:

___ Anita jumped in surprise.

___ The dog looked sad.

___ His head turned at the sudden noise as a motorcycle rounded the corner.

___ The beach was deserted.

___ Nausea overcame her as she read his words.

___ The flag snapped in the wind.

___ "Where's that sizzling coming from?"

___ The restaurant was huge.

___ Moira ran her fingers through his thinning hair.

___ *Crack.* I knew I shouldn't have put the glass bowl into the oven.

___ Her tan suede jacket and beige chemise contrasted beautifully with her dark-brown skin.

___ "Ew! What kind of cheese is that?"

___ It was October.

___ Steve and Tom ate the pizza, which was spicy.

___ Brooke threw the shirt at her husband. "Your girlfriend can wash this."

___ Malik opened the front door. It was going to be a hot one.

Worksheet

Exercise: 5-4

Identify and Replace Described Emotions

Circle described emotions in the following passage and then provide some substitute phrases that show, rather than tell.

> Bev was angry. She had heard the baby cry out and sensed that the child's mother didn't care. Bev suspected that the mother had hurt the baby and felt that someone should tell the nurse. As she heard the nurse open the hospital door and greet the new mother, Bev felt a chill.

_____

_____

_____

_____

_____

_____

_____

_____

_____

_____

Evaluate Your Writing
Show, Don't Tell Checklist

- ❏ I showed characters' emotions rather than just telling readers about them.

- ❏ I broke up any large blocks of description and instead conveyed the information through action and dialogue.

- ❏ I showed character traits through action and dialogue.

- ❏ I showed characters reacting to the weather instead of just describing it.

- ❏ I avoided explaining things to readers that I already showed through action and dialogue.

- ❏ I searched for filter words such as "saw," "felt," and "heard" and instead conveyed the sensation directly.

Chapter 6

THE ENDING

A good ending satisfies the reader, is in keeping with the story's genre and mood, makes sense and is plausible for the characters and the story, contains a bit of a surprise or a revelation, and is not too predictable.

Even in a short story, take a little time with the ending. Time doesn't necessarily mean length, but you should have enough of an ending that it doesn't feel as though you're dropping the story like a hot casserole lid.

The ending can provide insight into the theme. It can surprise or shock the reader. It can show how the character has evolved. It can circle back to something at the beginning of the story. If the character has been transformed, don't stop at the transformation. Give us a peek at the results.

Allow readers to take a breath and come to terms with the ending. A satisfying ending makes readers want to linger. And take particular care with the final sentence.

Stay away from endings that are too pretty and buttoned down. Also stay away from "the moral of the story" endings. You don't have to tell the reader what it all means. The ending should resolve the central conflict. It doesn't have to answer every question, but it should satisfy the reader.

Ideally, the beginning of the story should forecast the end. Think of it like bookends—take a phrase, image, location, or action from the beginning of the story and echo it at the end. This technique works particularly well if there is clearly a change in the character or situation. The repetition can be the same or have an important difference (a new result, an object that was broken at the beginning is now fixed, a line of dialogue has changed to reflect the character's evolution).

Don't be afraid to leave something to the imagination. Winning stories have endings that go beyond the ordinary. Take the time to give your story the ending it deserves.

Great is the art of beginning, but greater is the art of ending.
-Henry Wadsworth Longfellow

Worksheet

Exercise: 6-1

The Ending True/False

__ An ending should tie up all the loose ends of the story.

__ The ending can echo something from the beginning of the story.

__ You should avoid surprising the reader at the end of the story.

__ The ending should provide a moral.

__ The main character should have changed in some way by the end.

__ You should give readers a little breathing room at the end to absorb what they've read.

__ A short story should have a happy ending.

__ If you are running tight on word count, the ending is a good place to economize.

__ The ending should be in keeping with the genre and mood of the story.

__ The ending can provide insight into the theme.

__ The ending should be satisfying to the reader.

__ The writer should take at least as much time with the ending as the beginning.

__ The ending should be plausible.

__ The ending is where you explain what your story means.

Worksheet

Exercise: **6-2**

Choosing an Ending 1

What are some elements you could draw from this opening to frame a satisfying end to this story? Write a few paragraphs using the elements you have chosen.

Your story opens with a scene in which your main character, Sue, is finding out she has cancer. As Doctor Khan is explaining image-guided radiation therapy, Sue is momentarily distracted by a bird chirping outside the window. As the story continues, Sue, who is an artist, has to come to terms with her diagnosis and whether it means she won't have time to achieve her goal of having her work accepted for a major gallery showing.

Worksheet — Exercise: 6-3

Choosing an Ending 2

What are some options for an ending?

Your story is a humorous tale about a dog that wins a Halloween costume contest. The owner was hesitant to enter, but her fiancé dared her to take part.

Worksheet

Exercise: **6-4**

Choosing an Ending 3

What are some options for an ending?

Your story is a poignant story of a veteran suffering from PTSD who is helped by a service dog. The dog has just suffered a traumatic injury, so the vet suddenly finds herself in the helping role.

_____
_____
_____
_____
_____
_____
_____
_____
_____
_____

Evaluate Your Own Writing
The Ending Checklist

- ☐ I ended the story in the right place.

- ☐ The ending is satisfying to the reader.

- ☐ I left something to the reader's imagination.

- ☐ I gave the reader time to come to terms with the ending.

- ☐ I tested the story on readers and asked them if the ending seems rushed.

- ☐ The style and substance of the ending matches the genre of the story.

- ☐ The ending is plausible but not too predictable.

- ☐ I looked for ways to echo something from the beginning of the story.

- ☐ The ending isn't too moralistic.

- ☐ I didn't explain the ending to the reader; I let it stand on its own.

Chapter 7

PREMISE AND THEME

The premise of a story is the idea behind it—the starting point. It could be a "what if?" scenario (what if a man who plans to jump off a building gets stuck in the elevator), a reversal (man bites dog), or a seemingly hopeless setup (star-crossed love). The premise may incorporate setting, plot, and characters, but boils down to what the story is about.

Sometimes the premise incorporates an argument or point of view—something the writer sets out to prove, such as that drugs are being overprescribed. The premise might be this: A man hastily marries and then learns that impulsivity is a side effect of a medication he is taking.

As you develop your premise, remind yourself that you are writing a short story. You must balance the need for an original, engaging plot with the reality that you just don't have the space for complex story lines with many characters.

Once you have formulated a story premise, you can test it on readers to determine if your story will be engaging. The premise can also help keep you focused as you write so you don't waste time by getting off track (story creep).

The theme of a story is its underlying message. A story shouldn't be a lecture or a sermon, but people like to find meaning, and they enjoy knowing that their time has been well spent. The meaning of a story is found in its theme.

Theme can figure prominently in the story, or it can be lurking in the background and require some thought on the reader's part to discover. The theme may be a lesson learned such as there's no place like home, the moral of the story such as crime doesn't pay, or a classic struggle such as man vs. nature. Sometimes a story also demonstrates a universal truth such as money can't buy happiness or mother knows best.

A symbol is a word, sign, or object that represents an idea. Symbolism can help tie elements together and create a more powerful effect. It is a way of connecting seemingly unrelated pieces and can also cause the reader to make connections to broader concepts.

Premise and theme create the basis of the story. They encompass what the story is about both on the surface (premise) and at its core (theme). Symbolism uses objects, characters, or events to represent concepts.

To produce a mighty book, you must choose a mighty theme.
-Herman Melville

Worksheet — Exercise: 7-1

Premise and Theme True/False

___ The theme of a story is its underlying message.

___ A symbol can help tie elements together for better impact and meaning.

___ Universal truths like "better late than never" have been overdone and should be avoided.

___ The premise can help you stay focused as you write.

___ The premise is the main idea of the story.

___ A story must have an obvious moral or lesson.

___ Dorothy learns self sufficiency in *The Wizard of Oz*. This is an example of theme.

___ A symbol incorporates setting, plot, and characters.

___ The meaning of a story is found in its theme.

___ A story can include an argument, opinion, or moral the writer wants to express.

___ The theme of a story is often not obvious on the surface.

___ A theme must be original.

___ A premise can start with a "what if?" scenario or a reversal of a common situation.

___ In the movie *Twister*, the antagonist and his team drive black cars. This is an example of symbolism.

Worksheet

Exercise: 7-2

Premise, Theme, or Symbol?

Indicate whether each of these is a premise (P), theme (T), or symbol (S):

__ A girl travels for a year and then returns home.

__ A girl travels a great distance only to find that what she was seeking was at home.

__ A woman wrestling with aging carries a piece of sea glass in her pocket.

__ People hear noises in their house at night and find a homeless person living in their attic.

__ A woman who lost a child watches her garden come alive in the spring.

__ Two people fall in love.

__ Two people from warring families fall in love, which unites the families.

Evaluate Your Own Writing

Premise and Theme Checklist

- ❏ I developed a one- or two-sentence premise.

- ❏ My premise is plausible.

- ❏ The premise interests readers.

- ❏ I created a plot that isn't predictable, shallow, or overly complex.

- ❏ There is an underlying message or universal truth to give readers something to think about.

- ❏ I avoided being moralistic and preachy.

- ❏ I wove the theme into the story by giving elements within the story greater meaning.

- ❏ I looked for opportunities for symbolism.

Chapter 8

STRUCTURE

Time Frame, Sequence, and Transitions

In a short story, you don't have the space to span centuries; you must focus. You can cover a larger span of time, but if you do, focus on one or a limited number of points in time and use flashbacks and flash forwards to add interest and fill in important dramatic scenes.

Most short stories follow a linear, chronological sequence. It's a logical progression for the story that is easy for readers to follow. For beginning writers, this structure is an ideal place to start:

1. Hook the reader. Set the scene and introduce the main characters. Give the reader a sense of the style, mood, and type of story. Establish the point of view and provide a little background to set up the conflict or complication to come. What does the main character want?

2. Present a complication that stands in the way of the character's goal. This might be an antagonist character or force that provides conflict, or an event that presents a threat.

3. Create a plausible resolution, while leaving something for the reader to think about.

You need a smooth transition from one scene to the next. The easiest way to indicate a break of time or space is to simply insert space or a graphic element to indicate a transition.

Another way to signal a change is to use a transitional phrase such as "later that day" or "the next morning." You can get more creative by indicating a jump without specifically referring to it. Phrases such as "she closed the now-empty cigarette pack" or "New York was surprisingly cold that April" can signal transitions.

Transitions can be opportunities to change viewpoint, but be sure to alert the reader immediately. This is often done by starting with the new viewpoint character's name. Transitions do not have to be long (in fact, they shouldn't be), but they are necessary to smoothly move your characters and your story forward, without leaving your reader behind.

A subplot can provide an interesting dimension, add conflict, or reveal information about characters in the story. Unfortunately, it is difficult to find room for a subplot in a short story, so unless there is a compelling reason for a subplot, you should focus on the primary story.

Making a Scene

Although you may think scenes are limited to the movies, experienced writers think in terms of scenes. A short story may only have a few scenes, but they are still critical for getting the reader wrapped up in the story.

A scene is a story in miniature—told in real time, seen as it occurs, in a specific place and time. It has characters, setting, conflict, and resolution. The key aspect of a scene is that *something happens*. And the thing that happens moves the story forward.

The structure and order of the scenes is essential to the telling of the story. Each scene leads to the next, as the main character moves toward the goal. Within the scene is an immediate problem that must be resolved.

When thinking in scenes, also think about the follow-up, or sequel, to the scene. That is where the character reacts to the scene and makes a decision that leads to the next scene.

You will still need some breaks between scenes to vary the rhythm and pace of the story and to give readers a chance to digest what has happened. This is where a little narrative can be useful. You also need a way to transition between scenes.

Flashbacks and Flash Forwards

Flashbacks can be used to show, rather than explain, what happened in the past. Flashbacks can be particularly helpful when you want to start the story in the middle of the action but need to fill in some of the background to provide context and meaning. They can also be used to show incidents from the past that are relevant to the present situation.

Choose flashbacks wisely. A flashback scene should add depth and dimension to a key character and be integral to the action, important to the plot, and dramatic in the telling. When you use a flashback, be sure to give the reader a warning so it is clear when the flashback starts and when it ends.

Remember that flashbacks break the narrative, so they also break the reading experience. For this reason, flashbacks should only be used to provide essential insights that enhance the story, show an entire scene (ideally displaying characters in conflict), and be witnessed in present time.

Active vs. Passive Voice

Active voice puts the subject of the sentence into action rather than have the subject just be something things happen to. To find passive voice, look for past-tense verbs such as closed or attacked, paired with forms of "to be" such as "were," "was," "is," and "are." The word "by" can also indicate passive voice. Passive voice is not wrong, but it can take the sizzle out of your story. Notice the difference between "the car was crushed by the truck" and "the truck crushed the car." Which is more dramatic, "the doctor was fired by the administrator" or "the administrator fired the doctor"? Search out and reword sentences that are in passive voice.

If it sounds like writing, I rewrite it.

    -Elmore Leonard

Worksheet

Exercise: **8-1**

Structure True/False

__ A short story should never have flashbacks or flash forwards.

__ After an appropriate transition, you can change time or place.

__ Transitions should be at least one paragraph long.

__ A graphic such as a series of asterisks can indicate a time or location jump.

__ Short stories often follow a chronological sequence.

__ Character actions can provide transitions.

__ Establish the point of view near the end of the story.

__ Short stories are generally too short for subplots.

__ Abrupt transitions can make a story more interesting.

__ Introduce the main characters near the beginning of the story.

__ Dialogue can indicate a transition.

__ Short stories usually cover a short span of time.

__ A change in season can indicate a time jump.

__ You should hook the reader by the middle of the story.

__ Actions that show time has passed can serve as transitions.

__ The main character having breakfast would make a good flashback.

__ A scene includes characters, setting, conflict, and resolution.

__ Passive voice is best for characters who are shy.

__ Flashbacks are written in present tense.

Worksheet
Exercise: 8-2

Conveying Information

For each one of these situations, indicate whether the information would be better conveyed as narrative (N), a scene involving action and dialogue (S), or a flashback (F).

___ Jim's dog has broken through the invisible fence and run into the neighbor's yard. He chases after the dog, realizing too late that his neighbor has just re-seeded his lawn. The neighbor is opening the door to tell Jim to get off the lawn when his own dog darts out and starts to chase Jim's dog around the yard.

___ Jerry's wife is on him again about his alcohol use. The argument is playing out in its usual way when she says something that triggers a memory. Once, when he was thirteen, his mother showed up unexpectedly at his school. She made a drunken scene that was very embarrassing for him.

___ Emma is a recent college graduate who has not yet decided on a career. Her degree is in art history, but she now realizes that wasn't the best choice for finding a job.

___ Selena has just found out that her boss used a report she created and presented it as his own work. She confronts him and says she has no problem with him presenting reports she has generated, but she wants him to credit her. He refuses and says that as long as she works for him, any work she produces is his to use as he sees fit.

___ Officer Smith is about to start his shift when he recalls the argument he had with his wife the night before.

___ Jasmine pulls into the parking space and stops to remember whether she unplugged the coffee pot before leaving the house.

___ A nurse notices an orderly doing something inappropriate and decides to confront him.

Worksheet

Exercise: **8-3**

Changing Passive Voice to Active Voice

Rewrite the following selections to eliminate passive voice:

Sam watched the shelf as it was jumped on by the cat. The cat had been named "Trouble" by its original owner. Sam heard a crash as a book was knocked off the shelf by the cat. "Trouble! Get down," Sam yelled. The door was opened by Martha, who sat down and covered herself with an afghan that had been knitted by her mother. "That cat was given away by its owner for good reason," Martha said. "This house will be destroyed by him before long."

The book was thrown down on the librarian's desk. "Being banned is what should happen to this book." The title was read by the librarian. "*Heidi*?" she asked. "What offensiveness is contained in *Heidi*?" "Don't ask me," was how the man responded. "You're the one with the dirty books!"

_____
_____
_____
_____
_____
_____
_____
_____
_____
_____

Evaluate Your Own Writing
Structure Checklist

- ❏ I created a logical sequence for the story.

- ❏ I used scenes, rather than narration, where possible.

- ❏ Any flashbacks or flash forwards are necessary and easy to follow.

- ❏ I provided clear transitions for any skips in time or place.

- ❏ It's clear where flashbacks start and stop.

- ❏ If I changed point of view, I provided a clear signal for the reader.

- ❏ I devoted more space to the most significant characters and scenes.

- ❏ I looked for passive voice and avoided it where possible.

Chapter 9

PACING

Short stories move at a faster pace, in general, than novels. There is no room for filler. Scenes and dialogue that don't advance the plot or provide character insights should be removed to keep the story on track. Every scene, character, and sentence should serve a purpose.

Things that control pacing include the following:

- Number of scenes and their lengths
- Dialogue
- Unspoken thoughts
- Word and sentence structure (and length)
- Transitions

Pacing affects suspense, humor, emotional impact, and engagement. If your pacing is too slow, you may bore (or lose) your readers. If it's too fast, you run the risk of exhausting them.

Different types of stories require different pacing. An introspective story will have more leisurely pacing than a thriller, but there still should be some rhythm and variation in pace. You can change the pace by including flashbacks or flash forwards, adding sections of dialogue, or shortening or lengthening scenes.

Action, narrative, and dialogue should work together to move the story along. Decide what should be shown and what can take place in the background. Don't skim over important scenes, and don't drag scenes out.

While each scene should have some tension, make sure the pivotal scenes have the most tension and the scenes on either side of them have significant—if subtle—tension of their own. Everything must advance the story, so be selective.

Check pacing by reading the story aloud or having others read it. Increase pace by cutting a scene to condense time, starting the story closer to the end, shortening sentences, removing some adverbs and adjectives, using active voice, adding dialogue, increasing action, and reducing explanation. Reduce pace by adding more narrative and details, lengthening sentences, including a flashback, reducing dialogue, adding a distraction or setback, or including thoughts and reflection.

> *I want to write so well that a person is 30 or 40 pages in a book of mine... before she realizes she's reading.*
>
> -Maya Angelou

Worksheet

Exercise: 9-1

Pacing True/False

___ Unspoken thoughts can be used to slow the pace of a story.

___ Humor is not affected by pacing.

___ Pacing can never be too fast.

___ A good way to check pace is to read the story aloud.

___ Short stories generally move at a slower pace than novels.

___ Different types of stories require different pacing.

___ Adding a flashback speeds up pacing.

___ Important scenes should generally be longer.

___ Pacing affects suspense.

___ One way to increase pace is to start the story at an earlier point.

___ Active voice generally slows pace.

___ Pace should remain the same throughout the story.

___ Action, dialogue, and narration should work together to move the story forward.

Worksheet

Exercise: **9-2**

Changing the Pace

For each of these, indicate whether the action would speed up (SU), slow down (SD), or have no affect (NE) on the pacing:

___ In a scene depicting a robbery, you write: Maria was scared. Nothing like this had ever happened to her. She knew the neighborhood had gone downhill but hadn't thought it was actually dangerous. *At least the kids aren't with me*, she thought, remembering the last time they had stopped at his fast-food joint.

___ You delete a sequence inside the car and instead start the scene after the characters have arrived at their destination.

___ You're knowledgeable about skiing, so you tuck in some information about the type of ski your character is using, and how its design evolved.

___ As your character leaves home, you show the cold by having him pull up the collar of his coat and breathe into his hands.

___ You have a character going to a job interview and show the character practicing her answers to anticipated questions.

___ In a story about a blind date, you mention the time and have the character look at the clock several times.

___ Instead of explanation, you add a bit of brisk dialogue to show that the marriage is being strained.

___ In a story about a school shooting, you show a student stop to play with a neighbor's puppy while on his way to the bus stop.

___ In a murder mystery, the detective reviews the list of cleared suspects and explains why each of them couldn't have done it.

___ For a scene in a garden, you describe the flowers so readers will be able to imagine the setting clearly.

Evaluate Your Own Writing

Pacing Checklist

- ❑ The pacing of my story matches its content.

- ❑ I checked to make sure I don't have unnecessary filler than slows the pace.

- ❑ My story has a nice rhythm with intense scenes, followed by short periods of resolution or reflection.

- ❑ The pace of my story isn't so slow that the reader becomes bored.

- ❑ My story has tension that builds through the story.

- ❑ The plot moves forward at a speed that maintains reader interest.

- ❑ I removed scenes and dialogue that don't advance the plot.

- ❑ Dialogue, narration, and action work together to move my story forward.

- ❑ The pace of my story isn't so fast and sustained that it wears my reader out.

Chapter 10

SETTING

The story's setting should be chosen with just as much care as the characters—not only the geographic location, but also the time of year, hour of day, specific location, and reason the characters are there.

Use setting to convey mood. It is not just a stage or a backdrop. Have the characters interact with elements of the setting; the reader should experience the setting through the character's senses and actions.

The other component of setting is the span of time and amount of space. Just as a short time period adds immediacy and tension, a small setting (all the events taking place in one constrained area) adds focus and intensity.

The objects in a scene are more than just set decoration; they can convey information. A character's office, kitchen, bathroom, or bedroom can tell us much about him or her. A character might eat on paper plates but have silver candlesticks. Her office might contain a gaming computer or be papered with vintage postcards.

Details make a setting come to life but be sure to use details that give the reader information. For example, we don't care what kind of pants the character wears unless it tells us something about the character or the setting.

> *Belief and reader absorption come in the details: An overturned tricycle in the gutter of an abandoned neighborhood can stand for everything.*
>
> -Stephen King

Worksheet

Exercise: **10-1**

Setting True/False

__ Where a story is set isn't all that important.

__ Setting involves more than just physical location.

__ Mood can be conveyed through setting.

__ Characters should be shown interacting with the setting.

__ Setting is best described through narration.

__ Enclosing or reducing the size of the setting can add intensity.

__ The objects in a scene can convey information about a character.

__ Setting should be fully described in the first paragraph.

__ Season of the year and time of day can be an important part of setting.

__ Writers should select details that give the reader insights about the character or situation.

__ The setting should fit the story.

__ Setting is simply a backdrop for the story.

Worksheet

Exercise: **10-2**

How Setting Affects Stories

For each of the following scenes, explain what effect the setting might have on the story.

1. A husband tells his wife that he suspects she is cheating on him.
   Setting A: Their bedroom

   _____
   _____
   _____

   Setting B: On the street in front of their house

   _____
   _____
   _____

   Setting C: Inside their car

   _____
   _____
   _____

2. A woman is thinking about her husband's death
   Setting A: A dark, rainy night, alone in her kitchen

   _____
   _____
   _____

Worksheet

Exercise: **10-2**

How Setting Affects Stories, continued

    Setting B: Christmas morning, in the living room with her young children

_____

_____

_____

    Setting C: A lunch with her friend in a fancy restaurant

_____

_____

_____

3. A man pitches an idea for a new product

    Setting A: A formal boardroom filled with executives

_____

_____

_____

    Setting B: The boss's office

_____

_____

_____

    Setting C: An elevator

_____

_____

_____

Worksheet

Exercise: 10-3

Conveying Setting Indirectly 1

Convey this information without specifically mentioning the weather, location, or time period. Consider using clothing, furnishings, props, actions, dialogue, sounds, thoughts, food/beverages, scents, emotions, plants/flowers, or tactile details.

It's a hot, muggy summer morning in the 1950s. Your character is in the small kitchen of an old farmhouse in a rural area of Alabama. She cares for her elderly mother, who is in another room.

Worksheet

Exercise: **10-4**

Conveying Setting Indirectly 2

Convey this information without specifically mentioning the weather, location, or time period. Consider using clothing, furnishings, props, actions, dialogue, sounds, thoughts, food/beverages, scents, emotions, plants/flowers, or tactile details.

A veterinarian has just arrived at her clinic in Seattle. The waiting room is packed with clients and their animals, most of whom are not happy to be there. Several people are in line at the desk, but nobody is behind the counter.

Evaluate Your Own Writing
Setting Checklist

- ❑ I chose a setting that is a perfect fit for my story.

- ❑ I used the setting to help establish mood.

- ❑ I conveyed the setting with action and dialogue as well as description.

- ❑ My characters interact with the setting.

- ❑ I researched the location to make sure the details are accurate.

- ❑ I conveyed the setting over the course of the story rather than in one info dump.

- ❑ My setting is specific in time as well as location.

- ❑ I used sensory details (sound, scent, touch) in addition to visual description to convey the setting.

Chapter 11

CHARACTERS

Choosing Characters

A short story cannot have a cast of thousands; there simply isn't room. By the time you introduce a few characters and have them really mixing it up, it's nearly time to start wrapping up the story. For this reason, most short stories have no more than three or four characters.

A place to start is with one main character and two supporting characters, at least one of whom is an antagonist (a character standing in the way of the main character's goal).

The main character should be someone your readers will care about. He or she does not have to be perfect (and shouldn't be—that would be unrealistic and will make the character harder for readers to identify with) but should be sympathetic and generally likeable. The main character is usually, but not always, the viewpoint character—the character whose viewpoint is used to tell the story. The viewpoint character should be a doer, not just an observer.

When you add secondary characters, consider contrast characters. Supporting characters help the viewpoint character find a solution to the problem, create conflict, or set the character on the wrong course. Develop these characters through actions and dialogue, revealing a bit of information each time.

All characters need to serve a purpose; otherwise, there's no reason for them to take up space. Characters should each have their own world, even if it's never shown to the reader. Look carefully at each character and make sure he or she must be in the story.

Create a worthy antagonist, not just a black-hat character. The antagonist should be a multifaceted character with his or her own desires, fears, and qualities, whether or not all are shown in the story.

Characters' mannerisms, body language, facial expressions, speech, reactions, and even physical details should not be static. Real people are a combination of shifting traits expressed in various ways and affected by changes in circumstances and surroundings.

Sometimes in short stories, characters have to serve multiple purposes. If you find that you have too many characters in your story, consider combining them in ways that make sense.

Watch for default descriptions and clichés or your own stock phrases. Don't fill your stories with stereotypes or characters that look too much alike. Make your characters as real and variable as the people you meet in the world.

> *One well-chosen physical trait, item of clothing, or ideosyncratic mannerism can reveal character more effectively than a dozen random images.*
>
> -Rebecca McClanahan

Character Names

Take the time to choose appropriate names for your characters and make the names easily distinguishable. A well-chosen name can help convey a character's essence, but a name is not a character. Differentiate your characters through dialogue and action as well as name. Make sure your character names are appropriate to the character's age, ethnicity, geographic location, and time period.

Character tags are a way to identify a character by a trait or physical characteristic. They are more than just random quirks; they tell the reader something about the character. A character tag might be a strong handshake to indicate confidence, or frequent combing of hair to show vanity.

Character tags can be drawn from gestures, physical appearance, voice, mental state, scent, verbal tic, body language, or other aspects of the character's look or behavior. They help readers tell one character from another and telegraph information important to the story. The tags should be repeated (sparingly), in slightly different ways, to be memorable without being obvious.

Attributes/Descriptions

Resist the urge to immediately tell readers everything about the character. Give the reader a few details that provide a general idea of the age, sex, and background of the character, but use actions and dialogue to show whether the character is neat or tidy, rich or poor, happy or sad.

Worry about personality traits more than physical descriptions. Show traits, don't just tell us about them.

Because you want your reader to be able to identify with—or at least sympathize with—the main character, the character should be at least somewhat likeable, but don't make the main character unrealistic. No one is free from flaws.

Negative traits shouldn't be so off-putting as to make readers lose interest in what happens to the character. Minor negative characteristics such as sloppiness, awkwardness, tardiness, and forgetfulness can be accepted, and even found endearing. There are also flaws that nearly everyone can identify with such as being klutzy, forgetful, or socially awkward.

Whether a character in your novel is full of choler, bile, phlegm, blood or plain old buffalo chips, the fire of life is in there, too, as long as that character lives.

-James Alexander Thom

Worksheet — Exercise: 11-1

Characters True/False

Determine whether each of the following statements is true or false:

__ The viewpoint character should be like a reporter—conveying all the facts.

__ Secondary characters should be described at length when they are first introduced.

__ Each character should have his or her own world with friends, family, problems, opportunities, and desires.

__ Every character should figure into the plot and affect the dynamics of other character interactions or create an action that alters the course of the story.

__ A character should change over time and through experience, based on the events, surroundings, and other characters.

__ Each character should serve a single function, for example comic relief or foil for the main character.

__ Character names that begin with the same letter, rhyme, or sound similar may confuse readers.

__ A character tag tells the reader something about the character.

__ Characters readers recognize, like the shy librarian and the macho handyman, make great secondary characters.

__ Giving your main character a strong negative trait like racism or cruelty to animals will make the character more believable and appealing to the reader.

__ The best way to introduce a character is to describe the character's appearance and major traits right away.

__ Dialogue can be a way to convey a character trait.

__ You should give flaws to all characters except the viewpoint character.

__ If you have too many characters, you may be able to have one character serve two purposes.

__ Some character flaws can be endearing and make a character more likeable.

Worksheet

Exercise: 11-2

Bringing Characters to Life

Take a character you're working with and describe a way you might do each of the following (use a favorite fictional character if you don't have one of your own):

1. Provide details or quirks that show individuality.

_____

_____

_____

2. Show the environment that surrounds the character, particularly the surroundings the character has chosen for himself or herself.

_____

_____

_____

3. Have your character fight for something important to him or her.

_____

_____

_____

4. Give your character a negative trait or flaw that makes the character real without turning off readers.

_____

_____

_____

5. Let the character show us who he or she is through unspoken dialogue.

_____

_____

_____

Worksheet

Exercise: **11-2**

Bringing Characters to Life, continued

6. Put the character into action—show us what the character does and how, from small mannerisms to heroic (or evil) actions.

_____
_____
_____

7. Show how the character reacts to other people.

_____
_____
_____

8. Have something unexpected happen to the character to show how he or she reacts.

_____
_____
_____

9. Show how other people react to the character.

_____
_____
_____

10. Let the character talk and thereby show us who he or she is with dialogue, manner of speech, vocabulary, and expressions.

_____
_____
_____

11. Show how the character analyzes information, forms strategies, and solves a problem.

_____
_____
_____

Worksheet

Exercise: **11-3**

Conveying Character 1

Using methods other than pure description, write a short piece that conveys some traits of a friend, work colleague, or family member.

Worksheet

Exercise: **11-4**

Conveying Character 2

Give the reader a sense of this character through dialogue, action, his thoughts, other character's reactions, etc. Avoid simply describing him with adjectives.

The character is a mature, slim, well-educated man who is quite fond of expensive clothes, shoes, and watches. As he gets ready for the Chamber of Commerce mixer at a local sports bar, he worries that he is overdressed, although he'd prefer that to being underdressed. He isn't fond of mingling, but he hopes to attract clients for his law practice. As he walks into the bar, he learns that to get people to mingle, the host is taping the name of one of the local businesses to each person's back. The attendees are supposed to ask each other questions to find out what business each of them has been given.

Evaluate Your Own Writing

Characters Checklist

- ❏ I chose my characters, especially the viewpoint character, carefully and consciously.

- ❏ I selected names that fit the characters and are easy for the reader to distinguish.

- ❏ My main character is flawed, but someone with whom readers will be able to identify.

- ❏ I limited the number of characters to those needed to tell the story.

- ❏ My characters—even the secondary characters—are multidimensional.

- ❏ I conveyed character attributes and descriptions through the character's thoughts and actions.

- ❏ All my characters are necessary and serve different purposes.

- ❏ I chose the right character for the viewpoint character.

- ❏ I have at least one secondary character to provide contrast.

- ❏ My antagonist is more than a stock villain.

- ❏ My characters' speech, body language, and mannerisms vary, depending on the situation.

- ❏ I provided my characters with motivation.

- ❏ I checked that the names of my characters are plausible for their age, time period, and other factors.

- ❏ I avoided stereotypes and clichés.

Chapter 12

POINT OF VIEW

Choose your point of view carefully. Point of view affects the way the story is told, the facts the reader is privy to, and the internal thoughts conveyed. The story is being told through a narrator, but you need to choose whether the narrator is a character in the story (the main character or a secondary character), someone observing the story, or you, the writer.

With first person (I, we, my), the author is telling the story or is telling the story as one of the characters. In first-person point of view, you are in one head and can create and maintain a distinct inner voice. You are limited to experiences, perceptions, and conversations that can be seen or be sensed by the narrator, but you can choose whether or not that narrator is a trustworthy source of information.

Use the first person if it's important that the reader know the thoughts and feelings of your character and if that knowledge is essential for setting up the conflict. Use it if the events of the story are best revealed through the eyes of the character and if the character is best revealed by telling the story from his or her viewpoint.

Remember that if you choose a first-person narrator, that character has to be present in every scene in order to be able to communicate it to the reader. There are devices you can use to insert information about events outside the narrator's sphere, for example reading about events in someone's diary or in a newspaper, overhearing people talking about an event, or having another character describe the event to the narrator, but if you find yourself relying on these techniques more than once or twice, you may want to reconsider the first-person narrator.

First-person present tense can be difficult to maintain but does provide a sense of intimacy and immediacy. The reader really gets to know the character. The first-person narrator can be evasive, can lie to other characters, and can lie by omission to the reader. The biggest advantage of first-person point of view is that it puts the reader in the story and in the thick of the action. The biggest drawback is that it is sometimes limiting to not have the benefit of seeing and being able to report on all pertinent events in the story.

Second-person point of view (you) is less common, and can be effective in the right story, but is tricky to pull off successfully. Second person can give an offbeat, eccentric tone to the story. The author speaks directly to the reader, and the reader becomes a character in the story.

In third-person point of view (he, she, they), the narrator tells the story and can be privy to all actions, conversations, and events in the story. The third-person narrator is telling the story from an observer's point of view, which can put the reader at a distance.

A third-person narrator is observing from the outside and so is not part of the action. The third-person narrator can have access to all the characters' backstories, actions, and thoughts. Within third person, you can choose an omniscient narrator (the author can enter the mind of any character) or limited point of view (author enters the mind of only one character).

The omniscient third person can provide contrasting points of view and offers the opportunity to switch characters (which can be useful in a novel but can be difficult to carry off within the confines of a short story).

In the limited third-person point of view, the narrator observes all but enters the head of only one character. Use third person if using first person limits your ability to demonstrate the weaknesses of the main character, or if the story needs to be told objectively.

Whatever you choose, you should be consistent, as it can be confusing to readers when the point of view jumps around. If you decide to tell the story from different points of view, make sure there is an obvious break at each change.

The character you use to tell the story through is the viewpoint character. The way the character experiences these events and how the character responds, reacts, and changes is usually at the heart of the story. The viewpoint character is not just the focus of the action; the viewpoint character is the emotional focus of the story.

When choosing the viewpoint, consider the character who has access to just enough facts and events to tell the story, while leaving a little to the imagination. Ideally, the character has an interesting backstory or manner, is a big part of the story, and is a person with whom the reader will enjoy riding shotgun. With a single viewpoint character, the story can still be told in first-, second-, or third-person point of view.

Establish the point of view and whose head you are inside immediately, so readers know who is telling the story. Reveal the character's thoughts and feelings so the reader gets into the character quickly. Head hopping (jumping from one character's thoughts to another's) is disconcerting and confusing to readers.

Just remember that your narrator can't provide information he or she doesn't have access to or give insights based on events the narrator wasn't present to see. The narrator can't observe things out of his or her field of vision (the back of her own head, for example) and can't describe things that an individual isn't able to describe (what he looks like asleep, his own death). The narrator is not privy to conversations, events, and activities he or she has not observed or heard about from other characters and can speculate, but not know, the thoughts and emotions of the other characters. Whatever you choose for your viewpoint, be consistent unless there is a reason to change point of view or tense, and even then, you should be consistent within the scene.

I almost always urge people to write in the first person. Writing is an act of ego and you might as well admit it.

-William Zinsser

Worksheet
Exercise: 12-1

Point of View True/False

___ Point of view affects the way the story is told.

___ Third-person point of view provides intimacy.

___ The viewpoint character is the character you use to tell the story.

___ The most common point of view used in short stories is second person.

___ Readers like stories in which the point of view shifts among several characters within a scene.

___ With a story told in first person, you cannot know what another character is thinking.

___ In limited third-person point of view, the narrator sees everything but only knows the thoughts of one character.

___ A writer must choose the point of view carefully because it affects the facts the reader is privy to.

___ The viewpoint character should never be the main character.

___ A first-person narrator must be present in every scene depicted.

___ If you switch to another viewpoint character to tell the same story, the account will likely change.

___ With omniscient third-person point of view you cannot know the thoughts of more than one character.

Worksheet

Exercise: **12-2**

Points of View

Connect the point of view to its characteristics:

| First person |

| This point of view provides an edgier feel, with a narrator that speaks directly to the reader. |

| Second person |

| This point of view allows you (with care) to provide insights from multiple characters and offers a bird's-eye view. |

| Third person |

| This point of view is ideal for intimate or emotional stories, ones with strong main characters, and memoirs. |

Worksheet

Exercise: **12-3**

Choosing Point of View

Choose a point of view (or try several) for telling this story and write it from that perspective.

Erin suspects that her husband, Luke, is cheating on her with someone they socialize with. She and Luke are at a cocktail party when the other woman and her husband arrive and join them. Erin has had too much to drink and keeps making suggestive remarks about the woman. The woman's husband is baffled. Luke just wants to get Erin to go home without making a scene.

Worksheet

Exercise: **12-4**

Finding Point of View Errors

Identify the following point of view errors:

When I smiled, I revealed a piece of spinach in my teeth.

She laughed to herself as Jake handed her a suitcase he had meticulously packed the day before.

Cameron watched me and thought about how close we had once been.

I looked out the window but didn't see the cat run by.

Bob came up behind me.

My face turned red.

Lakeisha thought about her daughter before answering me.

Worksheet

Exercise: **12-4**

Finding Point of View Errors, continued

I caught his eye and he turned.

_____

_____

Rachel came in after I went to sleep and pulled my blanket up.

_____

_____

Ted opened the letter and was shocked by what he read.

_____

_____

She recalled this happening before as she handed me the phone.

_____

_____

Jamal walked in but didn't notice I had turned the lights down.

_____

_____

"What did you say?" I asked, my eyes dilating with anger.

_____

_____

Evaluate Your Own Writing
Point of View Checklist

- ❏ I chose the best way to tell the story (first, second, or third person).

- ❏ The viewpoint character I chose is the one most appropriate for telling the story.

- ❏ If I'm in one character's head, I am conveying only things that character could know.

- ❏ I avoided head hopping.

- ❏ I showed the character's emotions, rather than telling the reader about them.

- ❏ If my story is in first person, the "I" character is different from me.

- ❏ My character's voice is consistent with his or her education, background, location, intelligence, and age.

- ❏ I kept the point of view consistent.

Chapter 13

DIALOGUE

Creating Realistic Dialogue

Dialogue is a way of showing conflict, revealing character traits, and drawing the reader into the story. What characters say and how they say it is key to a winning story. Dialogue should move the story forward, show something about the character, convey information, or some combination of these.

Natural-sounding dialogue has contractions, sentence fragments, incomplete thoughts, slang, and even poor grammar. Spoken language is less formal than written language, and each person doesn't say much at one time.

Read dialogue aloud to make sure it sounds realistic. In real life, people interrupt each other, question, pause, and react. They may cry, laugh, sneeze, hiccup, or choke up. Dialogue shouldn't just be people talking at each other, and it shouldn't just be a way to inject information.

Once you complete a section of dialogue, take a close look at your dialogue tags—the explanations tacked onto the ends of dialogue (he said, she whispered). Dialogue tags tell the reader who is speaking and are necessary only when it isn't clear who is talking.

In most cases, "said" is the preferred tag, even if it seems repetitive. Rare use of terms such as whispered, yelled, or shouted is also acceptable. Just remember that dialogue tags must be vocalizations—ways of speaking (shrieked, murmured, explained). Don't make mistakes like these: "I bet not," he laughed. "Not today," she frowned. You can't laugh or frown words.

Use bits of physical movement to augment the dialogue and control the pace.

You don't need to explain dialogue to your readers. Sentences like this detract from the drama of the story: "So that's it," he said in astonishment.

If you find yourself using an adverb with dialogue, check to see whether any explanation is necessary. If it is, try constructing the dialogue to convey the action. Instead of "he said angrily" use "he shouted." Or better yet, work action into the dialogue: "I've had it," he said, banging his fist on the desk.

Dialogue Among Characters

Each character should speak differently, and they shouldn't all sound like you. Speech reflects age, cultural background, geography, education, occupation, gender, social standing, and personality.

Use dialogue to convey information (location, weather, and characters' appearances) in short, vivid bursts rather than long, adjective-packed narratives. Use actions (he stomped the floor to shake the snow off his large, half-frozen feet) rather than sticking in explanatory text that reads like a weather report. And never have one character tell another something he or she would already know.

Dialogue without interaction is like actors doing a script reading. In real life, people move, touch each other, and interact with their surroundings while they are talking. People may be interrupted, lose their train of thought, change the subject, or suddenly remember something.

Where appropriate (viewpoint characters only), include unspoken dialogue. This can be done by breaking up blocks of dialogue like this: "I'm calling her now," Bob said. *What a mess.* "We have to decide sooner or later." You can also break up dialogue with bits of narration: "I'm calling her now," Bob said. It had been three weeks since he'd raised the issue with Sarah. "We have to decide sooner or later."

Unspoken Dialogue

Unspoken dialogue (thoughts, sometimes called internal monologue) can be a powerful way to convey a character's personality, mental status, feelings, and attitude.

Whenever you provide the thoughts going on in a character's head, remember to keep the thoughts in the same voice (vocabulary, style of speech, and manner) as the character's spoken dialogue. Thoughts should embellish and enhance dialogue, not duplicate it.

Unspoken dialogue can be a way to show a character struggling with a problem or being dishonest with another character. It can also be a way of sharing facts with the reader that are being withheld from one or more of the characters.

> *Dialogue should covey a sense of spontaneity but eliminate the repetitiveness of real talk.*
>
> *-Elizabeth Bowen*

Worksheet Exercise: 13-1

Dialogue True/False

__ Dialogue can reveal character traits.

__ Dialogue should be more formal than the way people really speak.

__ A dialogue tag is the "he said" or "she said" that follows characters speaking.

__ Never use contractions (we'll, let's, I'd) in dialogue.

__ In dialogue, it's OK to have grammatical errors.

__ Dialogue is a good way to convey character.

__ It's acceptable to use made-up words like "ginormous" and nonstandard words like "ain't" in dialogue.

__ Setting cannot be conveyed through dialogue.

__ Unspoken thoughts, inner dialogue, internal monologue, and unspoken dialogue all mean the same thing.

__ A good way to check dialogue authenticity is to read it aloud.

__ When "said" has been used already, find a synonym like "mentioned" to use in in its place.

__ Dialogue can reveal conflict.

__ Dialogue combined with action can add impact and control pace.

__ Characters' spoken and unspoken dialogue should be consistent with their backgrounds, education, culture, and other factors.

__ Long pieces of dialogue are a great way to provide backstory.

__ Dialogue tags must be vocalizations.

__ Characters should never interrupt each other in dialogue.

Worksheet

Exercise: 13-2

Correcting Dialogue Errors

What are some things you might change about this exchange?

"How are you today?" Mary asked.

"Fine," said John.

"I saw your sister, Helen, who is a teacher," said Mary.

"That's a surprise," John said in astonishment.

"She said to give you this book about bats, which is old and moldy but looks expensive. I think it must be very valuable," she exclaimed.

"That's what you think," he laughed.

"I hate loud restaurants." *If there's anything I can't stand it's loud restaurants.*

Worksheet

Exercise: 13-2

Correcting Dialogue Errors, continued

"I'm here for you," said Colin.

"I know," said Jen.

"No matter what," said Colin.

"It's just that Holly—" said Jen.

"Never mind Holly," said Colin.

_____
_____
_____
_____
_____

Worksheet

Exercise: **13-3**

Enhancing Dialogue with Action

Experiment with adding different actions to change the meaning of this piece of dialogue.

"I do love you," Doug said _____.

_____

_____

_____

_____

_____

_____

_____

_____

Worksheet

Exercise: 13-4

Unspoken Dialogue

Which of the following would be good opportunities for unspoken dialogue?

1. A man recalling what he had for breakfast

2. A woman lying to her husband

3. A man thinking about his former wife while talking to his current one

4. A forgetful woman remembering she needs a dental appointment

5. Showing a character's fear of heights

6. Providing information about something that happened to another character

7. Conveying a character's hopes for her child

8. Showing a character saying something but meaning something different

9. Conveying a character's backstory

10. Showing a character's expert knowledge about termites

11. Conveying the thoughts of a non-viewpoint character

Evaluate Your Own Writing
Dialogue Checklist

- ☐ I used dialogue, where possible, instead of narration.

- ☐ The dialogue seems like a real conversation (it doesn't sound stilted or unnatural).

- ☐ The dialogue tags I used are necessary and unobtrusive.

- ☐ All the dialogue tags are vocalizations.

- ☐ My characters sound different from each other, reflecting different backgrounds, education, and personalities.

- ☐ I combined dialogue with action where possible.

- ☐ The dialogue advances the story or reveals information.

- ☐ I resisted the urge to explain dialogue.

- ☐ I read the dialogue aloud to see if it sounds realistic.

Chapter 14

THE TITLE

Like the frame of a painting, the title should be designed to set the work off to its best advantage, not just label it. The title should set the stage for the story and be compatible with the style, imagery, and tone of the story. Don't give away too much and be economical with your words.

In rare situations, you may think of a wonderful title before you even start writing, but if that isn't the case, wait until you finish writing to choose the title. If you create a title and then try to write toward it, the story may take you in another direction, or you may unintentionally constrain yourself.

Spending time worrying about the title can delay your getting the story down and is unlikely to yield a satisfying result. Sure, you can (and probably should) come up with a working title just to have a way of referring to the project. But when the work is complete, go through the story carefully and see what comes to you. You will likely think of something better.

Options for titles include: a line of dialogue; an obscure term, phrase, object, or activity from the story; a well-known event or cultural reference; or a line or phrase from a poem or book.

Convey the content, style, or theme of the story, but don't be too obvious. And unless the irony is clear, don't give a humorous title to a sad story or a romantic title to a story without romance. A title that deceives the reader—unless done for obvious effect—will lead to a disappointed reader.

> *It isn't easy, coming up with book titles. A lot of the really good ones are taken.* Thin Thighs in 30 Days, *for example. Also* The Bible.
>
> *-Dave Barry*

Worksheet

Exercise: 14-1

The Title True/False

___ The title should explain what the story is about.

___ An obscure term from the story could be used in a title.

___ The title should be in keeping with the style and content of the story.

___ A title should never be fewer than three words or longer than six.

___ The title is an opportunity for the writer to talk directly to the reader.

___ It's a good idea to have a working title when you start writing.

___ A title should be as short as possible.

___ The title should provide the theme for the story.

___ You should choose a title before starting to write so you don't get off track.

___ Your title shouldn't give away too much.

___ A foreign term should not be used in a title.

___ A phrase from a poem might be used as a title.

___ The moral of the story should be its title.

___ A line of dialogue should never be used as a title.

___ An ending might pay off the title by giving the reader the information necessary to understand its meaning.

___ A title should never be ambiguous.

Worksheet

Exercise: 14-2

Choosing a Title 1

What are some possible titles for this story?

You know you shouldn't accept a third Tanqueray & tonic, but you're enjoying the attentions of this beachy lifeguard. Andy. Even his name is cute. So what if he's at least ten years younger than you—all the better that he doesn't seem to notice. You revel in feeling like a college girl, even though you're long past your sorority days. This is what you had hoped would happen on this weekend at the beach—this time away from the job hunt, the family responsibilities, and the monotony of monogamy, a.k.a. your marriage to Jack.

You only half-wish that Fran had stayed at The Starboard with you. Sure, this weekend wasn't so great so far, but this was supposed to be a reunion. Has it really been fourteen years since you and she were roommates at American University? You can't believe that time has rushed through your life as fast as your son Max used to tear down the hallway to escape a bath when he was a toddler. But fourteen years? You do the math. Max was born the winter after graduation, and he just turned thirteen in April. My God! Sometimes you forget, or at least try to forget, that you're the mother of a teenager.

You wish you hadn't thought of Max just now. What would your son think if he knew that Mom was weighing her morals vs. her needs? And at this moment, your needs are the larger of the two. You and Jack are "having problems," as the cliché goes. Jack's been distant, and you've been distant, and maybe the distance this weekend might be the cure. Or maybe not. At the very least, this weekend in Dewey will be a litmus test.

(excerpt from a story by Nancy Powichroski Sherman from *Sandy Shorts*)

_____

_____

_____

Worksheet
Exercise: 14-3

Choosing a Title 2

Your story features a Civil War soldier who is writing a letter to his girlfriend the day before a big battle. Check the best options for the title:

- ❏ A Civil War-era term that could have double meaning
- ❏ A phrase that lets readers know the soldier didn't survive
- ❏ "Letter from a Soldier"
- ❏ A phrase from the letter
- ❏ Reference to a concept such as hope, fear, or courage
- ❏ An ambiguous romantic phrase

Evaluate Your Own Writing
Title Checklist

- ❏ I replaced my working title with a title that will make people want to read the story.

- ❏ I chose a title that makes my story stand out.

- ❏ The title provides intrigue without giving away too much.

- ❏ I avoided being too literal.

- ❏ My title fits the genre, style, and tone of my story.

- ❏ My title is distinctive and memorable.

Chapter 15

EDITING

The Editing Process

There are three main types of editing. Developmental editing is editing for basic structure, logic, character development, and other large-scale issues. Copy editing is a line-by-line edit for grammar, punctuation, spelling, and other issues relating to the mechanics of the writing. Copy editors work with a style guide (*The Chicago Manual of Style* and the *Associated Press Style Guide* are two popular ones) to make sure your writing is clear, correct, and consistent.

Proofreading is a skill that seems like something anyone can do but is difficult to do well. Professional proofreaders can find errors that escaped dozens of critical readers, editing passes, and self-reviews and check for often-overlooked errors such as page numbers out of sequence, inconsistent character name, incorrect type font or size, and improper paragraph indent.

Self-Editing

Most writers overwrite. Strategic cutting creates a story that has more dramatic impact, is more enjoyable to read, and has more punch. Cut. Cut. Cut. Cut until cutting any more will make the story worse, not better. Every word should work; every sentence should be vital.

As you edit, it is wise to save versions of the document under different titles (adding the current date to the file name is an easy way to keep track). When using computers, you may be tempted to just keep editing the same file, but what do you do if you deleted a scene three weeks ago and now decide to put it back in? If you have saved earlier versions, it's an easy cut-and-paste.

As you review your story, mark areas that seem to drag and those that seem rushed or confusing. Flag dialogue that doesn't sound authentic. Highlight sections that should be moved or that seem redundant.

Print your story and cut it into scenes. This will allow you to move them around to check structure and test whether you can eliminate the opening scene (or move it later in the story) or take an exciting scene from later in the story and move it up to the front. Shifting the arrangement of scenes can increase the drama. Look for paragraphs or scenes that don't seem to add anything. Cut them out and put them aside. When you are finished, read the edited version and make sure there are no holes in the story. If you decide to change your mind, it will be easy to retrieve the sections you cut.

Read the manuscript out loud. This can help identify awkward sentences, unrealistic dialogue, poor sentence rhythm, distracting words or phrases, bad pacing, dull patches, and too much explanation.

> *Not that the story need be long, but it will take a long while to make it short.*
>
> -Henry David Thoreau

Developmental Editing

Developmental editing, sometimes called editing for structure or the content edit, is big-picture stuff, and that's why it comes first.

Start by making sure you started the story in the right place. Eliminate any throat clearing and get right to the action. Watch the transitions too. Cut scenes of characters traveling from one place to another (unless something important is going on). Tighten sentences, look for verbose dialogue, and eliminate paragraphs or scenes that don't advance the story.

Editing for point of view is essential and should be done carefully. Make sure the point of view you've chosen and the character whose head you are in is the right one for telling the story. Watch for any slips in who is reporting the action and whose thoughts the reader is privy to. Be particularly careful if you changed the point of view.

Look for logic and timing inconsistencies. If a character puts the beer in the refrigerator, don't show someone retrieving it from a cooler. If you start the story in spring and months pass, different plants are blooming, people are wearing different clothing, and activities may have changed.

Check your narration for unnecessary information (unless you are intentionally providing red herrings). Are you relying on large blocks of narrative to tell your story, rather than acting it out in scenes?

Stories that are too slight often garner a "meh" from judges and readers. These are stories in which the conflict is not big or important enough, the character isn't engaging enough, or there just isn't enough at stake to make people care. Look for a way to incorporate another idea, conflict, character, or twist. Maybe you can tap into a deeper theme.

When you think you're finished, here are some additional things to try:

1. Add something to the end of the story that connects back to the beginning.
2. See if there are some pieces of information you can keep from the reader to create surprise at the end.
3. Look for places to add humor (a funny word, awkward situation, character quirk).
4. Search for opportunities to add depth of meaning without being moralistic.

Copy Editing

Copy editing is where you look at your story line by line, checking every sentence, every word, and every punctuation mark.

Check for common errors, especially those that spellcheckers may miss, such as "to" instead of "too" or "your" instead of "you're." Look for words ending in "ly" to root out adverbs and words ending in "ing" (often gerunds or dangling participles). Those sentences can usually be rewritten using stronger verbs and nouns. Minimize adverbs and adjectives by choosing verbs and nouns carefully (instead of "he quickly pushed the long, thin, pointed metal stick into the large cube of marinated lamb," write "he skewered the kebob"). Maintain an active voice (she socked him in the face) rather than passive voice (his face was hit by her fist).

Don't beat around the bush. Instead of "at this moment in time," write "now." And while you are at it, get rid of clichés like "don't beat around the bush."

Be aware of your writing tics. Every writer has them—a word you use too much, a phrase you tend to repeat, or a punctuation mark that pops up repeatedly. This is also the time to look at the structure of paragraphs and sentences. Do your sentences vary in length and style? Identify and remove redundant words.

> *Cut out all those exclamation marks. An exclamation mark is like laughing at your own joke.*
>
> *-F. Scott Fitzgerald*

Proofreading

Errors in grammar, spelling, and punctuation pull the reader out of the fictional world and brand the author as an amateur.

Read every word. Examine every little thing. Look for errors of the mind (where you said "stake" but meant "steak" or even "state"), formatting errors (an extra space or line, for example), and inconsistencies. If you changed a character's name, make sure you caught every one.

Proofread carefully to see if you any words out.

-Unknown

Worksheet
Exercise: 15-1

Editing True/False

___ The three main types of editing are: developmental editing, copy editing, and proofreading.

___ Copy editing includes recommending scene rearrangement or other structural changes.

___ Style guides go beyond grammar rules to include recommendations for consistent formatting, capitalization, and abbreviations.

___ Copy editors also do developmental editing.

___ A good way to check story structure is to cut it into scenes and move them around.

___ Developmental editing involves correcting grammar, spelling, and punctuation.

___ Automatic spellcheckers and grammar programs are always correct.

___ During editing you should check for commonly confused words such as peek, peak, and pique.

___ Proofreading is the first step in editing.

___ Most writers have a writing tic—a word, phrase, or punctuation mark they use too much.

___ A good way to check rhythm and pacing is to read the manuscript out loud.

___ Proofreading includes checking for inadvertently omitted words.

___ Most manuscripts just need proofreading.

___ Grammar, spelling, and punctuation mistakes can pull the reader out of your fictional world.

Worksheet
Exercise: 15-2

Types of Editing

Which type of editing deals with each of these items? Write "DE" for developmental editing, "CE" for copy editing, or "PR" for proofreading.*

___ Incorrect type size

___ Poor ending

___ Page heading incorrect

___ Point-of-view error

___ Removing incorrect apostrophe in "it's"

___ Redundant word or phrase

___ Time-inappropriate character

___ Incorrect dialogue tag

___ Need for more conflict or another setback

___ Spelling error

___ Character name wrong in two places

___ Changing where story starts

___ Incorrect spelling of "their" as "they're"

___ Incorrect italics

___ Wrong page number

___ Clichéd or overused phrase

___ Scene out of order

___ Inside wrong character's head for point of view

* Note that errors missed during the developmental edit or copy edit may be caught by the proofreader, and a developmental editor may flag a typo. For this exercise, indicate where the primary responsibility lies for detecting the error.

Worksheet

Exercise: 15-3

Identifying Writing Errors

Identify the problem with each of these sentences:

1. He woke up sick as a dog.

2. Damn! It was her turn! He was sick of it! He vowed to get revenge!

3. The train stopped at the station in Albany. She was unfamiliar with it.

4. "That's my coat," she laughed.

5. The carpenter looked at the various sizes of nails and chose the he thought would work best.

6. "It's a really big house," he said loudly.

Worksheet

Exercise: **15-3**

Identifying Writing Errors, continued

7. Cindy stood up and blinked her eyes. She put her PIN number into the ATM machine that was in close proximity to her house. The bank had offered a free gift for new customers.

   _____

   _____

8. Marsha put her paper dolls away. It was time to go to see *Frozen 2* with her parents.

   _____

   _____

9. "Their's nothing in here," he said, peaking into the box.

   _____

   _____

10. "I'll get right on that," said three-year-old Carol. "It's right in my wheelhouse."

    _____

    _____

11. He walked slowly.

    _____

    _____

12. "Where is it?" he bellowed. "It's behind you," she explained. "Thanks," he acknowledged. "You're welcome," she conceded.

    _____

    _____

Worksheet
Exercise: **15-3**

Identifying Writing Errors, continued

13. The clock chimed as I slept.

14. *I thought about it and decided to pick her up later.*

15. They consider chocolate a health food because its full of antioxidants.

16. The movie was better than anyone in audience had expected.

17. "I hope your feeling better."

18. His favorite television show was was "The Masked Singer."

Worksheet

Exercise: 15-4

Redundancy

Identify what is wrong with the following excerpts:

1. "It's you!" she said. "I'm so excited to see you! You've always been my best friend!

2. 8 a.m. in the morning

3. It was snowing. White flakes fell from the sky.

4. It was red in color.

5. The ring was really unique.

6. It was an unexpected surprise.

Worksheet

Exercise: **15-4**

Redundancy, continued

7. We had no advance warning.

8. She had gotten big as a house.

9. When it first began.

10. She learned she had the HIV virus.

11. That's a small speck of dirt.

12. Be there at twelve noon.

13. That was the end result.

Evaluate Your Own Writing

Editing Checklist

- ❏ I considered hiring a professional editor.

- ❏ I understand how developmental editing, copy editing, and proofreading differ.

- ❏ I eliminated scenes or blocks of dialogue that do not advance the story.

- ❏ The point of view stays consistent throughout my story (unless it's intentional and I have indicated a break).

- ❏ I eliminated redundant words, phrases, and sentences.

- ❏ I checked for overused words and phrases and my own writing tics.

- ❏ My sentences vary in length and style.

- ❏ I deleted trite phrases and clichés.

- ❏ I checked my manuscript for common errors.

- ❏ I had a proofreader go over my story.

Chapter 16

FACTS, LOGIC, AND LAWYERS

Fact-Checking

Research and fact-checking are essential for fiction as well as nonfiction. Research your location, time period, and other details using authoritative sources. Study the climate, landscape, styles of homes, and traffic conditions for any locations you reference in your story. Use the correct terminology for medical, technical, or specialty occupations or processes described in your story. You won't want to use all the research, but you will write more confidently as a result of knowing the information.

Errors pull readers out of the story and raise questions about the veracity of your writing. Confirm every date, address, name, specialized term, foreign phrase, historical detail, and fact. If you use a specific time and place for the story, verify that your seasonal and weather details are accurate. Check the spellings of street names, cities, and other details. Don't assume anything.

Logic

When you write a story, you are creating a fictional world and have the wonderful power to manipulate reality. But remember: Once you set the rules, you must be consistent. One of the writer's jobs is to maintain a sense of plausibility that allows the reader to step into—and stay within—the world you create.

The illusion can be shattered in any number of ways: an abrupt change in point of view, a logic error, an erroneous description, grammatical or spelling errors, or writing that calls attention to itself.

Make sure your stories don't sound dated. The writer's frame of reference affects many of the details within a story. If you are an older writer who is writing a story that takes place in present day, make sure to check names, prices, salaries, car models, medical terms, slang and popular expressions, and other details to make sure they are current.

Legal Issues

Intellectual property, like any other kind of property, is owned by a person or company, so another person or company can't just take it and use it. Written works, even if unpublished, are owned by the writer. Published works are owned by the copyright holder, which is usually, but not always, the writer. This means that, while you own the rights to your own work, you give up those rights if you sign a contract that gives the ownership to someone else. It also means that you cannot use another person's work without permission. This includes poems, lengthy quotations from books, song lyrics, and portions of film or movie scripts. And it includes written material on the internet.

The only works like these you are free to use are those in the public domain, which usually means that the work is old enough that the copyright has expired. Never assume that because something is on the internet it's in the public domain.

An exception is "fair use," which has to do with what type of material you are using, how you're using it, how much of it you're using, and whether your use deprives the copyright holder of income. Do some research before assuming your use would be considered fair and remember that owning a copy of the work is not the same as owning the rights to the work.

Most writers base their characters, at least in part, on people they have known, but they combine attributes, change identifying details, or otherwise disguise the descriptions so the individuals are no longer recognizable. Be cautious when using real people in your writing, even if they are friends or family members. You should not use a real individual's name, photo, or identifying information without permission. Even if the depiction is positive, you can get into trouble for using someone's likeness, name, or identifying information for commercial purposes. This is true even if that person is dead.

Public figures have less expectation of privacy than the average person. That said, celebrities have reputations to protect and lots of money for attorney fees, so if you do get sued, you can end up spending a serious amount of money defending yourself, even if the lawsuit is baseless.

> *Litigation: A machine which you go into as a pig and come out of as a sausage.*
>
> *-Ambrose Bierce*

Worksheet Exercise: 16-1

Facts, Logic, and Lawyers True/False

__ Fact-checking is not required if the story is fiction.

__ Quoting song lyrics is fine as long as you cite the songwriter's name.

__ Writers should take great care when using real people as models for characters.

__ Material on the internet is not copyrighted so it can be used.

__ With fantasy or science fiction, you are free to create any reality you want, as long as the rules are consistent.

__ Using several paragraphs of a poem would probably be considered fair use, as long as you don't quote the entire poem.

__ It's usually not necessary to check details on a story that takes place in current time and a well-known place.

__ Real people can be used as characters in a book if their names are changed.

__ Because restaurants are open to the public, a fictional story about someone getting food poisoning at a real restaurant would be acceptable.

__ Quoting a single sentence from a novel (and giving credit) would probably be considered fair use.

__ Trademarked brand names are legally protected, but they can be used if they are capitalized and not shown in a negative way.

__ When using a flash forward, you should check the timeline to make sure character ages and other facts are correct.

__ It would be OK to publish an old diary you bought at a thrift store.

__ A factual error can pull the reader out of the story.

__ Individuals have a right to privacy that extends to not being written about without their permission.

Worksheet

Exercise: **16-2**

Checking the Facts

Circle things in the following paragraph that should be verified.

Marlene Williams ate her raisin bran before asking her mother if she could go to a friend's house after school. Her friend lived on Oak Street, only a few blocks away from Gramwood Elementary School in Memphis. It was warm for February and they'd be getting a long weekend for Martin Luther King Day. She gazed out the window, past the camelia blossoms, to the condo building across the street. A city bus had just pulled up in front of the building and an elderly man was getting out.

Worksheet

Exercise: 16-3

Fact-Checking Resources

Match the fact with a reputable source for verification:

How to spell a word

Whether a building has a thirteenth floor

Whether the first name for a character born in 1910 is plausible

Whether to capitalize "army"

How many people live in a city

When the word "menthol" came into use

Whether a house built in 1890 still exists

The mission of a charitable organization

The proper spelling of a brand name

Whether there are cases of tuberculosis in the United States

What time the sun set on a day in 1983

Social Security Administration website

Wikipedia

Style guide such as *The Chicago Manual of Style*

Visit or interview with reputable local source

Neighbor or friend

Website or printed material provided by the company or organization

Government (.gov) website

Almanac (www.almanac.com)

Dictionary

Evaluate Your Own Writing

Facts and Logic Checklist

- ❏ I verified every fact.

- ❏ I checked and rechecked dates, names, spellings, figures, and other details.

- ❏ I used reliable sources for my fact-checking.

- ❏ My character names, dialogue, setting, and details are true to the time period (even if the time is current).

- ❏ The world portrayed in my story is logical.

- ❏ The timeline of my story makes sense.

- ❏ If I used copyrighted material, I got written permission or made sure it's fair use.

- ❏ If I used technical, medical, or other specialized terminology, I verified that it's accurate.

- ❏ I confirmed that any weather descriptions are plausible for the story setting (place and time).

- ❏ If I mentioned plants or animals, I verified the names and that they could exist in my story's time and place.

Chapter 17

MARKETING SHORT STORIES

Identifying Markets

For writers wanting to publish, one of the most difficult challenges is getting the attention of an agent or publisher. How does one stand out from the thousands of competing manuscripts? Well, one way is to find a niche.

A variety of different kinds of niches like these are available to writers:

- Geographic (city, state, region)
- Interest group (pet owners, veterans, parents of disabled children)
- Genre (mystery, steampunk, historical romance)
- Reader age (toddler, young adult, senior)
- Style/format of writing (novella, short story, flash fiction)

Ideally, the niche you choose connects with an area of expertise or strong interest, or a topic you are willing to research extensively.

Writing to a niche means consciously considering marketing, but not destroying your writing for the sake of marketing. You can take the story you planned to write and set it in a specific place (geographic targeting) or incorporate an issue or theme with specialized appeal.

A niche can help you identify outlets for your story. For example, a story geared toward older women might be marketed to senior-oriented magazines. A fictional historic story might be sold to a historical society magazine or be submitted to a historical fiction anthology.

Theme is another way to target a niche. If you plan to self-publish a collection of your own short stories, you may want to consider organizing the stories around an appealing theme or popular genre. Readers like stories that have a connection, whether that connection is a character, setting, style, or subject matter. Targeting a niche gives you a thread to tie the stories together *and* a marketing advantage.

Magazines

If you want to submit to a magazine, research the subscriber base to determine the publisher's interests and preferences. Review past issues to get a feel for what they publish. If you are writing for a contest, read the stories that won in previous years.

Magazines, journals, and anthologies that accept submissions all have guidelines for writers. Guidelines generally state what genres, lengths, and types of stories they use and offer insights to their criteria for selection.

Contests and Awards

Contests and award competitions can be a relatively easy way for a beginning writer to gain publishing credentials. Contests force you to read guidelines and write to a deadline and word count, which is good practice for becoming a professional writer. They also give you experience with editing, revising, and proofreading your work. Contests are generally inexpensive to enter, and if you win, you may get money, publication, or both. They also provide a chance to have your writing evaluated objectively. Publication gives you credibility as a professional writer and adds to your bio for future projects.

There are some dubious contests, so it pays to do a little research. Start by determining who is running the competition. Is the company or organization running the contest or offering the award legitimate? Is it a nonprofit organization hosting a contest primarily for its members? A profit-making company looking to create a commercially viable book? A vanity (pay-for-publication) publisher seeking new clients? An organization wanting to recognize literary merit? A writing services company wanting to sell coaching, editing, or publishing services? Poke around online and ask fellow writers about their experiences.

What is the purpose of the contest or award? Be wary of awards programs that have dozens of entry categories, each accompanied by a high fee. If the reward is publication, verify that the winning stories from previous years were published and examine the quality of the publication. Make sure that the contest is not simply a way to get people to pay to submit content that the organization can make money from without any benefit to you. Be wary of contests that promise literary agency representation (which may be the same company under another name) or require the purchase of their editing services. A contest for short stories should only require you to grant onetime (or first-time) publication rights. You should still own your story.

Evaluate the cost of entering the contest. Weigh the cost of the contest against both the value of winning and the odds. Is the award a recognizable honor or something no one ever heard of? Are winners required to receive their awards at a conference (which they must pay to attend)? Does everyone "win"? The prize should not depend on the number of entries received and should not require additional purchases. Be wary of a free contest that is run by a profit-making organization.

Examine the contest guidelines. Any legitimate contest will post the guidelines online or make them available on request. Stay away from contests that are vague about their guidelines or make them difficult to access.

How are the entries judged, if they are judged at all? Look for judging criteria, judges' names (or at least their positions), and judges' credentials. Make sure that past contests have resulted in a published book (if that is what is promised) and that any promised prizes have been awarded. A legitimate contest organizer should be willing to supply this information.

How to Submit

Submitting a story, whether to a contest or a publisher, is a business transaction. Submit using the vehicle requested (email, postal mail, online form) and include (unless the guidelines request otherwise) a polite, but brief, cover note that explains what you are submitting and what you are submitting it for (contest or publication). A line or two about your background is helpful, if it is pertinent (writing credentials, especially if similar publications, awards received, education).

Use a professional email address. Many writers maintain a separate email address for their writing so they can keep those communications separate from their personal email.

Submit a professional-looking manuscript that is as free from errors as possible. Manuscripts that look amateurish or have obvious mistakes will distract readers from what may be a winning story.

Before you hit "send," read the guidelines again and make sure you have followed them exactly. Deadlines, word counts, and formatting instructions are rules, not suggestions. Manuscripts that don't meet the guidelines are often not even read.

Worksheet

Exercise: 17-1

Marketing Short Stories True/False

___ Take care where you submit because short stories can only be sold once.

___ Contests can be a good way for a writer to practice the submission process.

___ If your goal is publication, it's a good idea to research potential markets before you even begin writing.

___ Magazines and journals generally specify the length of short stories they accept.

___ Writer's guidelines are helpful, but you shouldn't treat them as rules.

___ When submitting to a special-interest magazine (such as *Woman's Day*), you can improve your chances by submitting a story outside that interest.

___ Knowing the audience of the publication you're submitting to can be helpful.

___ If your story deals with a topic or interest (knitting, for instance), publications devoted to that subject may be good submission opportunities.

___ A contest prize of editing services may be a red flag that the company is trying to sell its services rather than run a legitimate contest.

___ When you submit to a publisher, it helps to have a cute email address such as iloveunicorns@gmail.com.

___ Most publishers don't care if submissions have grammar and spelling errors because they have editors who can fix them.

___ Writing to a niche means choosing a specific category such as sailing or older-adult romance and writing a story that fits to increase the odds of acceptance.

___ When you submit your story, it's a good idea to have a cover letter in which you say that, although you don't like to read and hate short stories, you've always wanted to be published and your kids think your story is really great.

___ The more expensive it is to enter a contest, the more likely it is that the contest is legitimate.

___ If a magazine only accepts flash fiction, you can submit a 5,000-word short story if it's really good because the magazine's editor could probably cut it down to the proper length.

___ If the writer's guidelines specify submissions by mail, it's still a good idea to send a few emails or make calls to see whether they've made a decision yet.

Worksheet
Exercise: 17-2

Why Would You Want to Enter a Contest?

Check the reasons you might choose to enter a writing contest.

- ❑ To gain a publishing credential
- ❑ To earn enough money to retire
- ❑ To help sell books you've written
- ❑ To get in an anthology that isn't very good, but at least your work will get published
- ❑ To help get other things you've written published
- ❑ To get your writing on the internet
- ❑ To gain exposure for your writing
- ❑ To pay off your student debt
- ❑ To get experience writing to a word count, editing, and submitting
- ❑ To win a discount for a book coach
- ❑ To get a lot of work out there so chances of success are increased

Worksheet
Exercise: 17-3

Contest Red Flags

Circle the signs that might be cause for concern.

1. The contest is run by a literary agency, and the prize is representation.

2. There is no entry fee.

3. The contest has multiple categories for novels but none for short stories.

4. The entry fee is low.

5. The contest is open only to students.

6. The prize money depends on the number of entries.

7. The entry fee is excessively high.

8. The contest has twenty categories for short stories.

9. You notice that the same contest is being run under different names.

10. The contest is run by a company you've never heard of.

11. A friend entered the contest last year and now gets lots of emails promoting publishing services and products.

12. You get repeated unsolicited email promotions for the contest.

13. The prize is a credit toward or discount on products or services.

14. The registration form requires you to agree to publication without compensation.

15. A company runs multiple contests simultaneously or a contest every month.

16. The award is a trophy or plaque that you must pay for.

17. You can't find any guidelines or criteria for judging.

Worksheet
Exercise: 17-3

Contest Red Flags, continued

18. The contest is run by a publishing company.

19. The company seems focused more on soliciting entries than on the awards themselves.

20. The contest's deadline is a year or more out or gets postponed with no winners announced.

21. Winners are required to buy copies of the anthology.

22. The contest is being run for the first time.

23. There is no apparent human involvement (generic email address, online payment, no contact information on website or no website, emails with questions go unanswered).

24. You must sign a contract assigning all rights to the publisher.

25. If you win, there will be additional costs (critiques, editing, agency fees, etc.).

26. The registration form asks for information such as social security number, mother's maiden name, or scan of driver's license or passport as proof of identity.

27. The prize is publication.

28. The contest is limited to writers in a certain region, of a certain age, or with a specific ethnicity.

29. The prize is publicity or a marketing package.

30. The sponsor reserves the right to substitute prizes, delay prizes for insufficient entries, or reduce prizes if certain conditions aren't met.

31. The terms and conditions are vague or confusing.

Worksheet

Exercise: 17-4

Understanding Guidelines

Read the guidelines below and then answer the questions that follow.

Tempting magazine is seeking submissions of short fiction (300-2,000 words) that deal with temptations (food, drink, shopping, activities). Our audience is women and men (3-1 women to men), aged 34-65. We do not accept sexually explicit material or stories that shame or preach. We are in need of stories from all parts of the United States, particularly out-of-the-way areas. Submit manuscripts using the link below. No simultaneous submissions, please. We buy first rights only.

1. Should you submit a poem to this magazine? ____

2. Should you submit a 1,500-word article about how the brain reacts to temptation? ____

3. Should you email your submission? ____

4. To stand out, would it be good to send a 250-word story? ____

5. Should you submit a racy romance? ____

6. Should you submit a story about two millennials who meet on a gaming site? ____

7. Should you submit a story for children about the temptation of candy? ____

8. To stand out, would it be good to send a story that takes place in Alaska? ____

9. Should you submit a story about a woman who loves smoking and how she deals with lung cancer? ____

10. Should you send a story about a man who loves cigars who meets a woman who loves cigars? ____

11. Should you submit a 1,700-word story about a cat that loves to swim in the ocean? ____

Worksheet

Exercise: **17-4**

Understanding Guidelines, continued

12. Should you submit a story about an eighty-year-old woman? ____

13. Should you submit a story about the bistros of Paris? ____

14. Should you submit a story you sent to another publication, since you haven't heard from them? ____

15. Should you submit a story about women who own wineries in the United States? ____

16. Should you submit a story that has already been published in another magazine? ____

17. To stand out, would it be good to send a 320-word story about a company that ships oysters from an island in Maryland? ____

Chapter 18

PUTTING IT ALL TOGETHER

We've covered story structure, premise and theme, characters, setting, dialogue, editing, fact-checking, and marketing. You've had a chance to practice what you've learned and apply it to your own writing. Now, here's an opportunity to bring together what you've learned so far.

A professional writer is an amateur who didn't quit.

-Richard Bach

Worksheet

Exercise: **18-1**

Match Terms with Definitions

Match each word or phrase with its definition:

Viewpoint character

Backstory

Telling detail

Writer's guidelines

Unspoken thoughts

Show, don't tell

Filter words

Bookending

Theme

Hook

Conflict

Pace

Flash forward

Scene

Flashback

Point of view

Copy editor

Spellchecker

Raise the stakes

The varying speed at which the story moves forward

What a character is thinking (also called unspoken dialogue or inner dialogue)

A publisher's rules for accepting a writing submission

A character's or situation's background and what led up to this point in the story

A situation conveyed in real time that contains characters, setting, conflict, and resolution, and that moves the story forward

An engaging element, often at the start of a story, that captures the reader's interest

The place from which the story is told, usually one of the characters or a narrator

An account of an event that took place in the past, written in present tense, that returns to present time at its conclusion

The underlying message of the story

Words that separate the reader from the emotion

Increase the danger, conflict, or importance of a goal

An illuminating detail that provides insight into a character or situation

A time skip to a future point, conveyed as a scene, with a return to present time at its conclusion

Echoing an object, line of dialogue, situation, or other element from the beginning of the story at the end

Use action and dialogue instead of narration

An internal or external pressure on the character that makes the reader care about the story's outcome

Person who corrects mistakes in grammar, spelling, and punctuation

Automatic editor, which may or may not be correct

Character through which the story is told

Worksheet
Exercise: 18-2

Match Terms with Examples

Match each word or phrase with an example:

Genre	Science fiction
Dialogue tag	When the negotiator arrived, he learned that his wife was one of the hostages.
Publication outlet	A veteran finds it difficult to deal with his son's interest in online war games.
Passive voice	
Transition	He said
Premise	The Joker from the Batman series
Antagonist	Flower buds opening to signal regeneration
Raise the stakes	Later that same day…
Personality flaw	The door was closed by Sally.
Symbol	A character's inability to empathize with others
	A literary journal

Worksheet Exercise: 18-3

The World's Worst Short Story

Using the skills you've learned, identify problems with this story:

A Birthday Story

Kaylee Hernandez was born in the hills of Foreston, Illinois. She had two brothers. She also has a sister. She has brown tresses and brown eyes. Today is her sixteenth birthday. She will be big for her age. She had a happy childhood. *I am so lucky*, she thought to herself. *I am too,* thought her sister.

One day, Kayli went to the store. The brakes were slammed on by her when she parked. She got out of the car quickly.

"Are those tomatoes on sale?" she asked quizzically.

"Yes!" laughed the store manager. "They are Nigerian-grown and shipped on dole container ships to Philadelphia, where they are off-loaded and transferred to flat-bed trucks."

"I love tomatoes!" exclaimed Kayley ecstatically.

"Me too," said the store manager.

Now that she is eighty, Kayly knows their are more ways to celebrate a birthday then they're used to be!

Then she woke up. It had all been a dream! That's when she realized that there's no place like home.

Worksheet

Exercise: **18-3**

The World's Worst Short Story, continued

Evaluate Your Own Writing

Pre-Submission Checklist

__ My story concept is original or a twist on a familiar tale.

__ The premise is plausible.

__ There is an underlying message that gives readers something to think about without being preachy.

__ The title is intriguing and coveys a bit of the story without giving too much away.

__ The first few sentences hook the reader.

__ The story starts in the right place (no throat-clearing).

__ The story contains tension and conflict.

__ The setting is specific and conveyed with sensory details.

__ Characters names and actions are appropriate to the time period and age of the character.

__ The main character is engaging and is likeable to the degree that the reader cares about him or her.

__ The characters have sufficient motivation to make the story plausible.

__ I presented significant events in the story as scenes with dialogue rather than just description.

__ Dialogue is realistic and appropriate to the characters.

__ Dialogue tags are appropriate and used only where needed.

__ The story does not fall back on stereotypes or clichés.

__ Viewpoint is consistent and any changes in viewpoint are easy for the reader to follow.

Evaluate Your Own Writing
Pre-Submission Checklist (continued)

__ Telling details convey mood, setting, character, and emotions.

__ I removed unnecessary explanations or replaced them with action and dialogue.

__ Any flashbacks or flash forwards are necessary and not confusing to the reader.

__ The pace of the story is just right.

__ Transitions are smooth and skips in time or place are clear to the reader.

__ The story ends in the right place.

__ The ending leaves the reader with a sense of satisfaction and enough time to enjoy it.

__ The story is a good match for the target publication.

__ The story is free from potential liability (use of copyrighted material, for example).

__ I removed extraneous or repetitive sections to tighten the story.

__ I replaced unnecessary filter words such as "felt" with words that convey the experience directly.

__ Where possible, I replaced adverbs and adjectives with stronger verbs and more specific nouns.

__ Using reliable sources, I verified all specific locations, terms, historical details, and other facts.

__ I checked the story for typos, grammatical errors, and writing tics such as overuse of exclamation points.

Answer Key

Answer Key

Exercise: **1-1**

Characteristics of Short Stories True/False

TRUE In short stories, the writer must telegraph information rather than provide lengthy explanations. **Wherever possible, convey setting, character attributes, and backstory through actions, dialogue, and the selection of specific nouns and verbs, rather than rely on adjective- and adverb-heavy description.**

FALSE Short stories usually provide complete backstories that explain how the characters came to be who they are. **Include only the backstory necessary for understanding the characters' actions and, where possible, convey it through dialogue or action.**

FALSE Short stories have less drama and impact than novels. **Because short stories are tightly focused, they often have intense drama.**

FALSE Readers are usually willing to give short stories more time to get started. **Readers expect short stories to progress quickly.**

TRUE Short stories usually have fewer characters. **Most short stories have one to three characters.**

FALSE The ending of a short story should tie up all the loose ends. **Short stories tend to be more open-ended than novels, although readers expect to feel a sense of satisfaction at the end.**

TRUE Complicated ideas and complex plots lend themselves better to novels than short stories. **If you are struggling to keep the story inside a short story word count, look to cut some scenes, a character or two, and any flashbacks or subplots. You may find you now have a tighter, more intense short story. However, if the story suffers instead of being improved, it may be better as a novel.**

FALSE Short stories often cover a longer span of time. **Although short stories can skip forward or backward through flashbacks and flash forwards, they generally follow a tighter, more linear timeline, and many take place in real time.**

Answer Key
Exercise: 1-1

Characteristics of Short Stories, continued

TRUE In short stories, there is even less room for unnecessary detail and for nouns and verbs padded with adjectives and adverbs. **A good editing exercise is to review each adjective and look for a stronger noun (large house=mansion). Likewise, examine each adverb and look for a stronger verb (walked slowly=strolled).**

FALSE Short stories are essentially the same as novels; they're just shorter. **Short stories differ in many ways, and although some writers practice with short stories, they often find that there are too many differences. It's like saying riding a bicycle is practice for driving a car. Yes, there are some similarities, but the vehicle, and how it behaves, is quite different.**

Answer Key Exercise: 1-2

Choosing What to Write

What should you write? Check any of the following that apply:

__ I use a lot of imagery and poetic language in my writing.

Consider memoir, historical fiction, or literary fiction.

__ I like surprise endings.

Consider mysteries, thrillers, or flash fiction.

__ I love to analyze relationships and tend to use a lot of dialogue.

Consider romance, bromance (male partners like Sherlock Holmes and Dr. Watson), or psychological thrillers.

__ My background is journalism or nonfiction writing.

Consider creative nonfiction, historical fiction, essays, or biographies.

__ I have a short attention span and get eager to move on to the next project.

Consider flash fiction and genres with light plots (e.g. romance).

__ My characters tend to be complex and have rich emotional lives.

Consider literary fiction, first-person narratives, or memoir.

__ I have lots of ideas for stories.

Consider flash fiction or series (connected short stories).

__ I like to have a theme that is woven into the story.

Consider literary fiction, memoir, or creative nonfiction.

__ My stories tend to have only one or two characters.

Consider literary fiction or strong protagonist/antagonist stories.

__ I love using flashbacks to fill in backstory.

Consider romance, memoir, or mysteries.

__ My stories tend to have multiple settings.

Consider travel stories, coming of age, or nonfiction forms.

__ I like to get right to the point.

Consider essays and other nonfiction forms.

__ I like to tell stories from multiple points of view.

Consider a novel, with each chapter from a different character's point of view.

Answer Key

Exercise: 1-2

Choosing What to Write, continued

__ I love world building (creating a fictional universe with its own societies and rules).

> **Creating a new world takes time and space. This is best suited to a novel (and probably a lengthy one or a series).**

__ I like family sagas that show multiple generations of the same family.

> **These kinds of stories are best told in longer form, but you could consider a series of linked short stories.**

__ I like to work quickly and get the job done.

> **You may be happier writing short forms, where you can see the results of your efforts relatively quickly.**

__ My writing tends to be concise (not filled with description, narration, complex relationships).

> **You may find you enjoy writing short stories, but also consider nonfiction.**

__ I love planning, outlining, mapping, and other organizational activities.

> **Some novel writers plan every element in advance (plotters) and some fly by the seats of their pants (pantsers), but if you enjoy extensive planning, you should consider a novel or nonfiction.**

__ I like to share in-depth information about my occupation, hobby, or special interest through my characters.

> **Consider writing novels or nonfiction.**

Answer Key   Exercise: 1-3

Should You Write Short Stories?

__ I like to experiment with my writing.

Short stories are a great way to try different subjects, genres, and styles of writing.

__ I love the research part of writing.

Although short stories also involve research, novels generally require much more.

__ I would rather work on many short projects than commit to one long project.

Most writers find it easier to juggle several short stories than to work on several novels at the same time.

__ I have lots of ideas.

Lucky you! Writing short stories may provide a way for you to develop more of them.

__ I like stories that are told in real time or over a short span of time.

Although some novels follow a linear timeline, that format is much more common in short stories.

__ I like to write stories with complex themes and multiple story lines.

In general, this type of writing is more conducive to longer works.

__ I have more energy than patience.

While any type of writing requires both, writing a novel can mean sticking with a single writing project for many months or even years.

__ I have a short attention span and get eager to move on to the next project.

You may be happier writing short stories.

__ My stories tend to have large casts of characters.

You may be happier writing novels.

__ I like to get right into the action.

That will make you a good writer in any form but especially with short stories.

__ I have little uninterrupted writing time.

If you want to write a novel, you may find a greater need for long periods of concentration, both for getting enough writing time in to complete a novel, as well as for retaining a solid memory of what you have written and where you plan to go.

Answer Key

Exercise: 1-3

Should You Write Short Stories, continued

__ I can't decide what to write because there are so many things I'd like to write about.

You may find short story writing more satisfying.

__ I have developed a character or group of characters I really like.

You should consider writing a novel or a collection of linked short stories.

__ I'm not sure what kind of writing I want to do (mysteries, thrillers, romance, etc.).

Writing short stories will allow you to try your hand at each.

__ I like to pit one character against another.

Ideal for a short story.

Idea Grid (example)

Starting Point	Where to Use	Impact	Possible Twists	Research Needed	Setting Options
Inner Fear: *Failure*	Character A worries about doing a good job.	Character A becomes despondent after getting fired.	Character A meets soulmate in unemployment line.	How people with fear of failure react to losing a job	Unemployment office
Dream: *I met an old crush*	Character B runs into an old boyfriend	Character B decides she'd rather be with old boyfriend	Character B finds out crush never had interest in her	Time for a woman to still recognize an old boyfriend?	Class reunion
Memory					
Discovery					
My Expertise: *Opera*	Business trip scene	Character C is on a tour with business associates	Character C stuns colleagues by singing an aria	Which opera halls have tours; which aria?	European opera hall
My Experience					
Motivates Me					
Emotional Trigger					
Person I Know					
Place I've Been					
Something Funny					
Common Problem					
Conflict					
Deadly Sin					

Potential Outlets: Submission Grid (example)

Outlet	Type of Pub	Genre Need	Words	Audience	Requirements	Deadline
American Short Fiction	Magazine	Contemporary Literature	<2,000	Discerning Adult Readers	Original, unpublished. Highly selective	September 1
Rehoboth Beach Reads	Contest Anthology	Any	500-3,500	Residents of and visitors to Rehoboth	Rehoboth setting, annual theme	July 1

Answer Key

Exercise: **2-1**

The Importance of Story True/False

FALSE One of the best ways to hook a reader is to start the story by describing the main character's background. **Action or dialogue would be more engaging.**

TRUE It's possible to convey some of a character's backstory through action. **Behavior can reveal upbringing, culture, and previous experience.**

TRUE The first few sentences of a story often determine whether a reader continues to read. **Try to engage the reader immediately.**

FALSE You should never open a story with a question. **It can make an intriguing start.**

TRUE It's important to ground the reader quickly by providing clues to the location. **Readers need a framework for the story unless mystery is essential.**

TRUE The best place to start a story may not be where you started writing it. **Clear away unnecessary throat clearing and get right to the action.**

TRUE Deciding where to start a story is one of the most important decisions the writer makes. **Where the story starts is key to guiding the reader's experience.**

FALSE It's important to describe the main character right away. **Not necessary.**

TRUE One way to convey backstory is with unspoken thoughts. **Can be effective.**

TRUE It's important to put characters in motion quickly. **Helps hook the reader.**

FALSE If you open the story with a question, be sure you answer it before moving on. **You can create suspense by withholding the answer for a while.**

TRUE It's OK to just write the story from the beginning, but when you're finished you should go back and make sure that's the best place to open the story. **A good practice to develop.**

FALSE You should never start a story with dialogue. **Dialogue can be an effective opening.**

FALSE A mystery story should always start with the murder. **Not necessarily.**

Answer Key

Exercise: **2-2**

Choosing a Story Opener

1. Dialogue between two men planning a crime

   Starting a story in the middle of a discussion like this can provide intrigue. Make sure it feels as if the reader has started to overhear a conversation in progress (don't reveal everything immediately).

2. Information about a historical event that is key to the story

   If this information must be told, weave it in later in the story. Unless it's necessary to the understanding of events in the story, consider providing it as a note at the end of the story.

3. A scene featuring a skydiver jumping out of a plane

   This could be an exciting start to a story.

4. A character describing his hobby

   Most readers won't be interested in this level of detail. Provide an interesting tidbit or two, but don't open your story with this kind of background information.

5. The recounting of an event that took place in an earlier time

   Not likely to engage the reader.

6. An exclamation such as "You've got to be kidding me!"

   The reader will want to know what was said before the story opens. A good hook.

7. Description of an operating room door closing

   Done well, this is a good start to a story. What happened? Who's in there?

8. Unspoken dialogue such as: *And yet again, I find myself saying yes.*

   Opening a story with unspoken thoughts immediately brings the reader into the viewpoint character's head and makes a compelling start.

9. Explanation of the relationship between the two main characters

   This is backstory that can be revealed later in the story.

Answer Key — Exercise: 2-2

Choosing a Story Opener, continued

10. A scene that shows a robot being constructed

    Unless it is written in an intriguing way (a race against the clock, an element of mystery) this is not a compelling opening.

11. Two characters having breakfast and discussing the day ahead

    If routine (no conflict or element of mystery), leave it out.

12. Description of the main character's appearance

    Not a good opening for a story.

13. Someone slapping another person's face

    A shocking start that will keep readers reading.

14. A question such as "What do you want?"

    Who has appeared? What is going to happen? An interesting start.

15. Explanation of how something works that is important in the story

    Detail that can either be left out or woven into the story later.

16. A child being kidnapped

    This could be an engaging scene that hooks the reader.

17. A woman making beef stew

    Unless something unusual happens or it's used as contrast (someone's screaming from another room), this would not be a good way to open a story.

18. An odd contrast such as a crow in a church or a clown asking a police officer for directions

    Situations that are difficult for the reader to interpret can inspire additional reading. Most people will want to understand what is going on.

19. Description of a Little League game

    Unless it's at a dramatic point that is key to the story (or provides an important character insight), probably not a good opening.

Answer Key — Exercise: 2-3

Knowing Where to Start

It was a warm day in September. Claire pushed her long blond hair off her face as she closed the door to her tidy Nantucket bungalow. She had lived on the island for six years, working as a copy editor for the local paper. As she got to her car, she noticed that the tires were flat.

Opening here would ground the story quickly (place, time, character, backstory) but is rather dull and unlikely to hook the reader.

Again. Claire gazed up the quiet Nantucket street. Her tires had been slashed for the second time in little more than a week. *This has got to stop.*

Opening with the thoughts of the main character gets the reader inside the head of the character instantly. We get the location (Nantucket) and the inciting incident (slashed tires) quickly.

Claire strode into the press room of the *Nantucket Gazette*, dropped her handbag and laptop at her workstation, and wheeled around the corner to confront Silas.

Opening with action gets attention and has readers wondering "what's going on here?" We still learn a little about the character and the setting and are also introduced to the antagonist.

"You're not going to get away with this." Claire glared at Silas, who gazed up from his computer with an annoyed expression.

"What's that then?"

"You know what. My tires are slashed. This has got to stop."

Opening with dialogue puts the reader into the scene immediately. We meet the main character and the antagonist, but don't know what they are talking about initially, which provides mystery.

Silas smirked. "It will stop when you stop slashing my copy."

Opening with Silas's explanation for the inciting incident may give a little too much away, but still provides some mystery (what copy? Why did she slash it?).

Answer Key
Exercise: 2-4

Converting Backstory 1

Dorothy's age and position in the family could be conveyed by her clothing, actions, or unspoken thoughts.

The setting could be conveyed through narration or through dialogue. Lisa could say something like "I wish you didn't live out here all by yourself."

Dorothy is eighty-five and matriarch of the family. She lives alone in the family home, a large farmhouse in rural Pennsylvania. Her sons, Don and Ed, want her to move into assisted living, but as someone who has always been in charge, she can't bear the thought. Her daughter, Lisa, has just arrived for a visit. Lisa's brothers want her to convince their mother to move but Lisa hates confrontations. She has problems of her own and feels she has never measured up to her mother's expectations.

When she arrives, Lisa's attitude and her mother's will be key to conveying how they feel about each other.

Since the brothers aren't here, you could introduce a letter, phone call, unspoken thoughts, or have Lisa bring this up in dialogue.

Consider using unspoken thoughts to convey Lisa's feelings or have her discuss them with her mother.

Answer Key

Exercise: **2-5**

Converting Backstory 2

Sherry's worries could be shown through unspoken dialogue.

Sherry and Mike's relationship, as well as his issues, could be conveyed through dialogue or even a flashback.

Sherry is an only child and her parents had high expectations for her. She is thirty-five and has been living with Mike for five years. He has had trouble keeping a job (he'd rather party), so she works as a waitress instead of finishing her degree. They recently bought a mobile home in Salisbury. Her parents are about to arrive for a visit. They wanted to surprise her, so the only warning she had was a call from the airport.

This phone call, combined with unspoken thoughts or dialogue with Mike, would provide rich opportunities to convey backstory.

Their home could be shown through actions and sensory details

The surprise visit offers a chance to show Sherry and Mike scrambling to tidy and prepare mentally (and possibly argue), which could convey information about them both.

Answer Key — Exercise: 2-6

Converting Backstory 3

Hopes and dreams can be shown in unspoken dialogue but also conveyed through objects (film posters) and actions (practicing in front of a mirror)

> Katie has moved to California in hopes of breaking into TV or film. She has the looks but not the connections. Years of dance, singing, and modeling lessons have prepared her for this moment. An inheritance has funded the move and provided money to cover about six months of living expenses. She feels a bit guilty, as she knows her brother really needs the money, but this is her big chance.

Financial situations can be conveyed through actions (budgeting), dialogue (phone call with brother), or thoughts.

The "big chance" raises the stakes and provides an opportunity to introduce an anticipatory dream, unspoken thoughts, or even an imagination-based flash forward.

Answer Key — Exercise: 3-1

Conflict True/False

TRUE A central conflict is an important part of a story. **It's essential.**

TRUE The central conflict can be something for the character to solve, overcome, or be consumed by. **It can also be internal or external pressure.**

FALSE To increase conflict, lower the stakes. **Raise the stakes to increase conflict.**

TRUE A time limit can increase tension. **Putting a clock on the action increases pressure on the character and provides tension for the story.**

TRUE A personality flaw can serve as an obstacle for a character to overcome. **A personality flaw such as a short temper or prejudice can make a character more interesting and be something for the character to work on during the story.**

TRUE Conflict propels a character into action. **It provides a reason for the character to move forward in the story.**

FALSE The pivotal scene (climax) of the story should be quick so the character can move on. **Because of its importance, the pivotal scene should be given extra attention and space.**

TRUE A character's decisions and failures should have consequences. **Failures give characters opportunities to learn, improve, and move forward. Punishment can provide motivation and a change indirection.**

FALSE Conflict must come from the outside (be external). **Conflict can be internal (a phobia, anxiety, religious beliefs).**

TRUE A moral dilemma is one type of conflict. **A character may struggle with whether to do the right thing or with whether to act at all.**

Answer Key — Exercise: 3-2

Identify Conflict in a Story

The Wizard of Oz

The main conflict is Dorothy's desire to get home. Obstacles in her way include a wicked witch, an inept wizard, beasts of the forest, deadly poppies, and a quest to get the witch's broomstick, the wizard's requirement for helping her get home.

Romeo and Juliet

The main conflict is that the lovers come from warring families. The feud puts significant obstacles between them.

Star Wars

This movie is a classic good vs. evil conflict, featuring Luke Skywalker's quest to become the Jedi Knight and save the galaxy against the Empire.

Gone with the Wind

Gone with the Wind has two basic conflicts: one between the willful Scarlett O'Hara and the old guard of the antebellum south and the other between Scarlett and Rhett Butler.

The King's Speech

In this movie, the new king must overcome a character trait (a stammer) to succeed in the age of radio.

The Hunger Games

In this man vs. society story, Katniss must find a way to survive and protect her family and friends despite society's requirement that she participate in the deadly games.

The Perfect Storm

A man against nature conflict is at the heart of *The Perfect Storm*, a fictionalized account of a real event—a fishing boat caught in a massive storm at sea.

Apollo 13

It's man against technology as the astronauts (and the team at NASA) deal with a mounting series of failures that threatens the mission and the lives of the astronauts.

Pride and Prejudice

The main characters (Elizabeth Bennett and Mr. Darcy) struggle with each other but also with society and its rigid expectations.

Answer Key

Exercise: 3-3

Create Conflict

It's more challenging to create conflict within the confines of a short story, but it can certainly be done. Consider the following description of a scene and suggest some possible sources of conflict and ways to convey it in a short story.

A couple is sitting at the breakfast table. The man is reading the newspaper and the woman is going over her day's schedule on her phone. They have two children. One is away at college; the other is upstairs, getting dressed for school.

Options

Breakfast. Start by imagining all the different food and beverage choices (bloody mary vs. a cup of strong coffee, eggs and bacon vs. a kale smoothie).

Body language, facial expressions, and actions such as lip biting can convey tension. Sounds other than speech—groans, moans, a nasty laugh—can change the dynamic of a simple scene.

Backstory, whether revealed directly at this point or not, can complicate relationships. Is the man the father of both children (and does he know this)? Are the children providing conflict? The relationships between each of the children and each of the parents will be different and one or more may be troubled. What has been happening with each of the children? Are either of them involved in conflicts of their own at school or with their friends? With a teenager, even the matter of dress can provide conflict. Suppose the child comes downstairs wearing a T-shirt with a provocative phrase or image? Is music playing? If so, whose choice was it and do the others like it?

Conflict Chart (example)

Conflict	Characters Affected	Stakes/Time Limit	Actions Taken	Obstacles/ Complications	Actions Taken	Results
Woman has affair	Husband	Marriage is at risk	Husband suggests couple's counseling	Wife refuses	Husband gets a divorce lawyer	Husband falls in love with divorce lawyer
Woman has affair	Woman	Must decide between husband and lover	Disappears for two days to decide	Still conflicted	Consults friend	Discussion is overheard
Woman has affair	Lover	If affair becomes public, he will lose job	Asks woman to leave husband	Wife refuses	Lover gets angry	Affair is reported, lover loses job

167

Answer Key — Exercise: 4-1

Details True/False

TRUE Details can reveal emotions. **A character's choice of food, companion, activity, or music could convey their frame of mind.**

FALSE A telling detail must be verbal (in dialogue). **It could be description or action.**

TRUE Telling details are precise and illuminating. **The more specific, the better.**

FALSE The best details are visual. **Details can involve any of the senses.**

FALSE Slang, regionalisms, and foreign terms should be avoided. **They can add richness.**

TRUE Details mentioned by a character should be in keeping with the character's age and background. **Otherwise they don't ring true.**

FALSE The best details are adjectives. **A specific noun is often better.**

FALSE Details should be included in description rather than in dialogue or action. **Details can be conveyed by any of those means.**

TRUE Research can help identify details to include in the story. **Look for telling details.**

FALSE A writer should avoid withholding information from the reader. **It can add tension.**

TRUE Telling details are more specific than general details. **Specific details provide insight.**

TRUE Details can convey inner character as well as physical appearance. **The best kind.**

TRUE The details a character chooses to mention can be revealing. **They can show prejudice, for example.**

FALSE Telling details must be technical or more complex. **Not necessarily.**

TRUE When choosing details, try to include different senses (sounds, smells, textures, etc.). **Including other senses can provide depth to the description.**

Answer Key Exercise: 4-2

Adding Details

Areas where you might have added telling details are highlighted:

Jillian **went** to her **grandfather's home**. She could hardly believe it had been **so long** since she had last been here. **Standing** in the **front yard**, she **noticed** how **run-down** the house was. The **columns** were **weather-beaten**. Above them were a **broken window** and **trim that was missing pieces**. **Her friend** had warned her Gramps' place was **looking rough**, but it was **worse than she expected**. Jillian had **suffered**, too. Moving back into **her childhood home** had seemed like a **good** solution, especially since Gramps would need **help** when he got **home**.

Here are the details author Lynnette Adair used:

> Jillian went to her grandfather's home early and alone. She could hardly believe it had been so long since she had last been here. Standing in the front yard, she absorbed the cockeyed, rotted shutter, disconnected from its window, drooping precariously and covering most of the panes. The columns on the verandah—once painted glossy white and as smooth as a pair of freshly shaved beach legs—now stood weather-pitted and weak, tired of holding up the porch roof. Above them, the jagged glass of a broken bedroom window hid in shame under a canopy of ivy. Fanciful gingerbread trim that used to evoke long-ago parties now mimicked the missing teeth in a seven-year-old's smile. Her lifelong best friend, Amy, had warned her Gramps' place was looking rough, but it had suffered much more than she expected. Jillian had suffered, too. Moving back into her childhood home had seemed like a good solution, especially since Gramps would need help when he got out of rehab.

Note how details can not only describe but also draw suitable comparisons. For example, this is a house by the sea, so the description of the columns as "smooth as a pair of freshly shaved beach legs" is apt and specific. The comparison will also resonate with the book's target audience: women.

Answer Key — Exercise: 4-3

Spot Mistakes with Details

Paul had brown hair parted on the side, blue eyes, and was of medium height.

These details are all visual and provide no insights to the character, setting, or situation.

On Emma's way to elementary school that morning, she noticed that the kousa dogwood trees had started to bloom.

Although mentions of specific plants is fine, they must be details that the character would be likely to know and notice. It's not plausible (unless explained) that a child would recognize and mention a specific type of tree.

World War II was coming to a close and the soldiers were happy to spend their free Saturday nights watching *The Ed Sullivan Show*.

Fact-check your details. The war was over by the time *The Ed Sullivan Show* began running, and when it did run, it was on Sunday nights.

Miranda bent down and picked up the *gumiszalag*.

Foreign terms are fine, but unless familiar to most people, they should be placed in a context that allows the reader to get some idea of their meaning.

Peggy ate another veggie chip and smiled at her Mommy. "I like these whatever-they-ares."

It's fine to show a character not knowing the name for something (a child wouldn't know the names for lots of things). The only error here is that "Peggy" is not a plausible name for a contemporary child.

The room had blue walls, two windows, a door to the kitchen, and a rug on the floor.

These details tell us nothing. Specifics and sensory (other than visual) details would enrich this significantly.

"This looks like a Migration Period sword, which was popular during the Merovingian period. It was derived from the Roman-era spatha and gave rise to the Carolingian sword of the eighth to eleventh centuries."

Just because you did the research (good for you!), you don't need to dump it all into a single sentence, especially if it's dialogue. No one talks like that.

Answer Key

Exercise: 4-3

Spot Mistakes with Details, continued

She pulled up in front of the very large house.

Details don't have to be adjectives. Sometimes a stronger noun is better (mansion).

"Hand me that Johnson screwdriver," said Meg.

There is no such thing as a Johnson screwdriver, so this is either an error or a clever telling detail about Meg (she is clueless about tools or often confuses names).

Answer Key   Exercise: 4-4

Creating Telling Details (examples)

Telling details are illuminating and provide insights beyond just being specific. Fill in the chart below.

General	Detail	Specific Detail	Telling Detail
Place to spend the night	Hotel	Ritz Carlton	Bridal suite
Place to eat	Fast food	McDonald's	Star Wars Happy Meal
Transportation	Car	Limo	Stretch Hummer
Clothing	Coat	Fur	Vintage mink
Pet	Puppy	Bernese Mountain Dog	Missing one leg

Answer Key Exercise: 5-1

Illustration vs. Explanation True/False

FALSE Narration is the best way to tell a story. **Dialogue and action can be effective.**

FALSE To bring characters to life, the writer should describe their emotions. **It's better to show them through action or unspoken dialogue.**

TRUE Setting can be described through actions. **Actions can convey weather, culture, time period, and other aspects.**

FALSE The clearest way to describe an emotion is just to state it: James was angry. **It's better to show it through action, dialogue, or a combination.**

TRUE Character traits such as kindness can be conveyed through action or dialogue. **How a character behaves and speaks can be revealing.**

FALSE "Show, don't tell" means to use description rather than dialogue or actions to convey setting or character. **It's the opposite.**

FALSE Weather is the only part of setting that can't be described through actions. **Weather can be conveyed by putting on a coat, opening an umbrella, or wiping sweat.**

TRUE Instead of stating that a character heard something, the author might include a sound effect or character reaction. **That would make it more lively for the reader.**

TRUE Using action and dialogue to convey situations helps provide a richer experience for the reader. **Stories that rely too much on narration or description can be dull.**

FALSE Personality must be described; it can't be portrayed through actions. **Actions can show a character's lack of control, love for animals, sense of humor, etc.**

FALSE To make sure readers understand, the writer should reinforce dialogue or actions through explanation. **That's redundant.**

TRUE "Felt" is one of the filter words that separate readers from the character's experience. **It is almost always better to show what was felt.**

Answer Key Exercise: 5-2

Show, Don't Tell

1. Hazel was old.

Examples:

Hazel rubbed her aging knees.
Hazel's reflection revealed lines and wrinkles.
Hazel touched her graying hair.

2. Bob was embarrassed.

Examples:

Bob's face grew hot.
"Bob, you're blushing!"
Bob couldn't maintain eye contact and shifted in his seat.

3. The house was big.

Examples:

The sound echoed through the expansive rooms.
Mary wondered how they removed cobwebs from ceilings that high.
The foyer was as big as her own living room.

4. It was a hot day.

Examples:

Dennis opened a window, hoping for the slightest breeze.
Sally's blouse clung damply to her back.
"This heat is enough to take your breath away."

5. Barbara was tired of Phil's lies.

Examples:

"I've had it with your lies."
"That's the last time you're going to lie to me."
Barbara slammed the door behind her—she would never have to listen to his lies again.

Answer Key — Exercise: 5-2

Show, Don't Tell, continued

6. Luke was a cheapskate.

Examples:

"I had a cheaper drink, so my portion of the bill…"

Luke rinsed out the baggie so he could use it again.

"Luke, don't you think fifty cents is too small a tip?"

7. She saw the car coming toward her.

Examples:

The sun's reflection on the hood momentarily blinded her as the car approached.

She stopped—the car was headed straight at her!

It was the headlights that caught her attention. "Oh, my God. Look out!"

8. He heard a whizzing sound as the bullet passed him.

Examples:

A bullet passed by with a whiz.

Whiz. The bullet had just missed him.

He ducked as the bullet whizzed by.

9. The cottage was near the ocean.

Examples:

Theresa could hear the sea when she opened the window.

Theresa swept sand off the mat and gazed toward the ocean.

"You are so lucky to be able to walk to the beach!"

Answer Key

Exercise: 5-3

Show or Tell?

Using an S or T, indicate whether the following show or tell:

<u>S</u> Anita jumped in surprise.

<u>T</u> The dog looked sad.

<u>S</u> His head turned at the sudden noise as a motorcycle rounded the corner.

<u>T</u> The beach was deserted.

<u>S</u> Nausea overcame her as she read his words.

<u>S</u> The flag snapped in the wind.

<u>S</u> "Where's that sizzling coming from?"

<u>T</u> The restaurant was huge.

<u>S</u> Moira ran her fingers through his thinning hair.

<u>S</u> *Crack*. I knew I shouldn't have put the glass bowl into the oven.

<u>S</u> Her tan suede jacket and beige chemise contrasted beautifully with her dark-brown skin.

<u>S</u> "Ew! What kind of cheese is that?"

<u>T</u> It was October.

<u>T</u> Steve and Tom ate the pizza, which was spicy.

<u>S</u> Brooke threw the shirt at her husband. "Your girlfriend can wash this."

<u>T</u> Malik opened the front door. It was going to be a hot one.

Answer Key — Exercise: 5-4

Identify and Replace Described Emotions

Circle described emotions in the following passage and then provide some substitute phrases that show, rather than tell.

Anger can be shown through an action such as slamming a door.

The sound of the cry might work.

Suspicions could be shown through thoughts or behavior.

Bev was angry. She had heard the baby cry out and sensed that the child's mother didn't care. Bev suspected that the mother had hurt the baby and felt that someone should tell the nurse. As she heard the nurse open the hospital door and greet the new mother, Bev felt a chill.

An action here could convey this.

An opportunity for a sound effect and dialogue from the nurse

She could be shown arguing with herself about what to do, texting a friend, or making a phone call.

Answer Key

Exercise: **6-1**

The Ending True/False

FALSE An ending should tie up all the loose ends of the story. **Leave something to the imagination.**

TRUE The ending can echo something from the beginning of the story. **A good option.**

FALSE You should avoid surprising the reader at the end of the story. **Surprises can be fun.**

FALSE The ending should provide a moral. **Not necessarily.**

TRUE The main character should have changed in some way by the end. **Otherwise, what's the point?**

TRUE You should give readers a little breathing room at the end to absorb what they've read. **Readers like time to appreciate the story in its entirety.**

FALSE A short story should have a happy ending. **The ending should suit the story.**

FALSE If you are running tight on word count, the ending is a good place to economize. **The ending is the worst place to cut things short.**

TRUE The ending should be in keeping with the genre and mood of the story. **Otherwise, you've misled the reader.**

TRUE The ending can provide insight into the theme. **It can help the reader find meaning.**

TRUE The ending should be satisfying to the reader. **An inadequate ending disappoints.**

TRUE The writer should take at least as much time with the ending as the beginning. **Both are key to a good story.**

TRUE The ending should be plausible. **Don't have readers shaking their heads.**

FALSE The ending is where you explain what your story means. **Let readers figure it out.**

Answer Key — Exercise: 6-2

Choosing an Ending 1

Your story opens with a scene in which your main character, Sue, is finding out she has cancer. As Doctor Khan is explaining image-guided radiation therapy, Sue is momentarily distracted by a bird chirping outside the window. As the story continues, Sue, who is an artist, has to come to terms with her diagnosis and whether it means she won't have time to achieve her goal of having her work accepted for a major gallery showing.

Here are some elements you could draw from this opening to frame a satisfying end to the story:

1. **Study image-guided radiation therapy and see whether it provides any potential parallels or opportunities for metaphor.**

2. **Consider whether a bird or the sound of a bird could figure into the ending.**

3. **The character is an artist who deals with imagery and the creative process. Consider how this could lead to a different way of coming to terms with her situation.**

4. **Is there any art in the doctor's office? Could that provide a point of interest or even humor?**

5. **The character may not achieve her goal of a gallery showing, but could you create a goal she could achieve by the end of the story?**

6. **There are multiple kinds of images in this story. Consider how you might use imagery as a theme and how it could lead to an ending.**

Answer Key

Exercise: **6-3**

Choosing an Ending 2

Your story is a humorous tale about a dog that wins a Halloween costume contest. The owner was hesitant to enter, but her fiancé dared her to take part. What are some options for your ending?

There is no right answer, but here are some options for your ending:

1. A funny twist—perhaps the dog won in an unusual way, chewed up or gave away its prize, or its owner won something as well.

2. What prize did the dog win? Perhaps it was an unexpected category.

3. Consider mentioning something at the beginning (a costume that was considered but rejected, a fear of something, an expectation of something, a prop) that you can repeat at the end.

4. Perhaps the fiancé has an unexpected reaction?

5. Maybe the contest isn't the end of the story. Perhaps something significant happened after the contest.

Answer Key

Exercise: **6-4**

Choosing an Ending 3

Your story is a poignant story of a veteran suffering from PTSD who is helped by a service dog. The dog has just suffered a traumatic injury, so the vet suddenly finds herself in the helping role. What are some options for your ending?

There is no right answer, but here are some options for your ending:

1. Consider ending with dialogue or unspoken thoughts from the veteran, as this is a personal story.

2. Is there a way to broaden the impact? Interaction with another vet or the owner becoming a dog trainer?

3. Going through another traumatic situation may have triggered memories or flashbacks. How might these impact the ending?

4. PTSD is complex, so avoid a simplistic happy-ever-after ending and indicate a future of continuing challenges.

Answer Key — Exercise: 7-1

Premise and Theme True/False

TRUE The theme of a story is its underlying message. **It's its point.**

TRUE A symbol can help tie elements together for better impact and meaning. **Symbols can be subtle but effective.**

FALSE Universal truths like "better late than never" have been overdone and should be avoided. **Universal truths resonate and can make good themes.**

TRUE The premise can help you stay focused as you write. **A premise can keep you on track.**

TRUE The premise is the main idea of the story. **It's what the story is about on its surface.**

FALSE A story must have an obvious moral or lesson. **If there is a moral, keep it subtle.**

TRUE Dorothy learns self sufficiency in *The Wizard of Oz*. This is an example of theme. **There are several themes in that movie, but self sufficiency is one of them.**

FALSE A symbol incorporates setting, plot, and characters. **That would be a premise.**

TRUE The meaning of a story is found in its theme. **Readers like a story to have meaning.**

TRUE A story can include an argument, opinion, or moral the writer wants to express. **Just don't lecture your readers.**

TRUE The theme of a story is often not obvious on the surface. **Let readers discover it.**

FALSE A theme must be original. **Themes are often familiar universal truths.**

TRUE A premise can start with a "what if?" scenario or a reversal of a common situation. **"What if" is a great way to spark an idea.**

TRUE In the movie *Twister*, the antagonist and his team drive black cars. This is an example of symbolism. **It was a modern version of black hats on cowboys.**

Answer Key

Exercise: **7-2**

Premise, Theme or Symbol?

Indicate whether each of these is a premise (P), theme (T), or symbol (S):

P A girl travels for a year and then returns home.

T A girl travels a great distance only to find that what she was seeking was at home.

S A woman wrestling with aging carries a piece of sea glass in her pocket.

P People hear noises in their house at night and find a homeless person living in their attic.

S A woman who lost a child watches her garden come alive in the spring.

P Two people fall in love.

T Two people from warring families fall in love, which unites the families.

Answer Key

Exercise: **8-1**

Structure True/False

FALSE A short story should never have flashbacks or flash forwards. **They can be useful.**

TRUE After an appropriate transition, you can change time or place. **Good transition is key.**

FALSE Transitions should be at least one paragraph long. **They can be much shorter.**

TRUE A graphic such as a series of asterisks can indicate a time or location jump. **An easy choice.**

TRUE Short stories often follow a chronological sequence. **Not always, but usually.**

TRUE Character actions can provide transitions. **For instance, getting out of a car.**

FALSE Establish the point of view near the end of the story. **Establish it much sooner.**

TRUE Short stories are generally too short for subplots. **A longer story may have room.**

FALSE Abrupt transitions can make a story more interesting. **They distract the reader.**

TRUE Introduce the main characters near the beginning of the story. **Ground the reader.**

TRUE Dialogue can indicate a transition. **"Traffic was terrible" can signal arrival, for example.**

TRUE Short stories usually cover a short span of time. **Many are told in real time.**

TRUE A change in season can indicate a time jump. **One way to convey time has passed.**

FALSE You should hook the reader by the middle of the story. **Hook the reader sooner.**

TRUE Actions that show time has passed can serve as transitions. **Closing a book, for example.**

FALSE The main character having breakfast would make a good flashback. **Dull unless significant.**

TRUE A scene includes characters, setting, conflict, and resolution. **A story in miniature.**

FALSE Passive voice is best for characters who are shy. **Avoid passive voice when possible.**

TRUE Flashbacks are written in present tense. **A previous event, told in present tense, is what makes it a flashback.**

Answer Key

Exercise: 8-2

Conveying Information

For each one of these situations, indicate whether it would be better conveyed as narrative (N), a scene involving action and dialogue (S), or a flashback (F).

S Jim's dog has broken through the invisible fence and run into the neighbor's yard. He chases after the dog, realizing too late that his neighbor has just re-seeded his lawn. The neighbor is opening the door to tell Jim to get off the lawn when his own dog darts out and starts to chase Jim's dog around the yard.

F Jerry's wife is on him again about his alcohol use. The argument is playing out in its usual way when she says something that triggers a memory. Once, when he was thirteen, his mother showed up unexpectedly at his school. She made a drunken scene that was very embarrassing for him.

N Emma is a recent college graduate who has not yet decided on a career. Her degree is in art history, but she now realizes that wasn't the best choice for finding a job.

S Selena has just found out that her boss used a report she created and presented it as his own work. She confronts him and says she has no problem with him presenting reports she has generated, but she wants him to credit her. He refuses and says that as long as she works for him, any work she produces is his to use as he sees fit.

F Officer Smith is about to start his shift when he recalls the argument he had with his wife the night before.

N Jasmine pulls into the parking space and stops to remember whether she unplugged the coffee pot before leaving the house.

S A nurse notices an orderly doing something inappropriate and decides to confront him.

Answer Key

Exercise: **8-3**

Changing Passive Voice to Active Voice

Rewrite the following selections to eliminate passive voice:

Sam watched the shelf as it was jumped on by the cat. The cat had been named "Trouble" by its original owner. Sam heard a crash as a book was knocked off the shelf by the cat. "Trouble! Get down," Sam yelled. The door was opened by Martha, who sat down and covered herself with an afghan that had been knitted by her mother. "That cat was given away by its owner for good reason," Martha said. "This house will be destroyed by him before long."

The book was thrown down on the librarian's desk. "Being banned is what should happen to this book." The title was read by the librarian. "*Heidi*?" she asked. "What offensiveness is contained in *Heidi*?" "Don't ask me," was how the man responded. "You're the one with the dirty books!"

There are several ways to correct these errors, but here is one approach for each:

Sam watched as Trouble, the cat, jumped up on the shelf and knocked off a book. *Crash*. "Trouble! Get down," Sam yelled. Martha opened the door, came in, and sat down, covering herself with an afghan her mother had knitted. "That cat's owner gave him away for good reason," she said. "Trouble will destroy this house before long."

The man threw the book on the librarian's desk. "This book should be banned." The librarian read the title. "*Heidi?*" she asked. "What is offensive in *Heidi?*" "Don't ask me," the man responded. "You're the one with the dirty books!"

Answer Key — Exercise: 9-1

Pacing True/False

TRUE Unspoken thoughts can be used to slow the pace of a story. **A character thinking aloud provides a pause.**

FALSE Humor is not affected by pacing. **Humor is all about timing.**

FALSE Pacing can never be too fast. **Fast pacing with no relief tires readers.**

TRUE A good way to check pace is to read the story aloud. **Or have it read to you.**

FALSE Short stories generally move at a slower pace than novels. **They are usually faster paced.**

TRUE Different types of stories require different pacing. **A thriller requires fast pacing while a family saga can take its time.**

FALSE Adding a flashback speeds up pacing. **A flashback is a break from the action.**

TRUE Important scenes should generally be longer. **Key scenes should be well developed.**

TRUE Pacing affects suspense. **Watch the movie *Jaws* if you doubt this.**

FALSE One way to increase pace is to start the story at an earlier point. **Cut to the chase to speed up the pace.**

FALSE Active voice generally slows pace. **Active voice speeds up pace.**

FALSE Pace should remain the same throughout the story. **Only if you want to bore the reader.**

TRUE Action, dialogue, and narration should work together to move the story forward. **They each contribute to the pacing.**

Answer Key

Exercise: 9-2

Changing the Pace

For each of these, indicate whether the action would speed up (SU), slow down (SD), or have no affect (NE) on the pacing:

SD In a scene depicting a robbery, you write: Maria was scared. Nothing like this had ever happened to her. She knew the neighborhood had gone downhill but hadn't thought it was actually dangerous. *At least the kids aren't with me*, she thought, remembering the last time they had stopped at this fast-food joint.

SU You delete a sequence inside the car and instead start the scene after the characters have arrived at their destination.

SD You're knowledgeable about skiing, so you tuck in some information about the type of ski your character is using, and how its design evolved.

NE As your character leaves home, you show the cold by having him pull up the collar of his coat and breathe into his hands.

SD You have a character going to a job interview and show the character practicing her answers to anticipated questions.

SD In a story about a blind date, you mention the time and have the character look at the clock several times.

SU Instead of explanation, you add a bit of brisk dialogue to show that the marriage is being strained.

SD In a story about a school shooting, you show a student stop to play with a neighbor's puppy while on his way to the bus stop.

SD In a murder mystery, the detective reviews the list of cleared suspects and explains why each of them couldn't have done it.

SD For a scene in a garden, you describe the flowers so readers will be able to imagine the setting clearly.

Answer Key — Exercise: 10-1

Setting True/False

FALSE Where a story is set isn't all that important. **It should be integral to the story.**

TRUE Setting involves more than just physical location. **It also involves weather, time period, and time of the day or year.**

TRUE Mood can be conveyed through setting. **A scene that takes place on a rainy night will be different from one that takes place on a sunny morning.**

TRUE Characters should be shown interacting with the setting. **It helps bring a scene to life.**

FALSE Setting is best described through narration. **Setting is best conveyed through action and dialogue in addition to narration.**

TRUE Enclosing or reducing the size of the setting can add intensity. **Watch Alfred Hitchcock's *Lifeboat*. The entire movie takes place on a small boat.**

TRUE The objects in a scene can convey information about a character. **Especially true of objects the character has chosen.**

FALSE Setting should be fully described in the first paragraph. **Provide some hints, but make the reader curious to read more.**

TRUE Season of the year and time of day can be an important part of setting. **Like weather, season and time of day can affect mood and character interaction.**

TRUE Writers should select details that give the reader insights about the character or situation. **Especially specific, illuminating (telling) details.**

TRUE The setting should fit the story. **A good match between story and setting is essential, even if that match provides intentional contrast.**

FALSE Setting is simply a backdrop for the story. **Setting should come alive and not just be in the background.**

Answer Key — Exercise: 10-2

How Setting Affects Stories

1. A husband tells his wife that he suspects she is cheating on him.

Setting A: Their bedroom

A bedroom setting provides not only intimacy but also sexual overtones that may add impact to the scene. Bedrooms are generally small, which adds tension. If there are other people in the house or if the couple lives in an apartment, they may have to keep their voices down. Either character could storm out of the room.

Setting B: On the street in front of their house

In this public setting the couple is likely to keep their voices down and restrict their body language unless either of them loses control. Cars may pass by, neighbors may be in their yards, or children may be playing nearby, all of which are possible distractions or concerns.

Setting C: Inside their car

The inside of a car is intimate and has the added element of containment. The two people are likely sitting next to each other. If the car is moving, neither can quickly leave, and the one not driving may feel imprisoned. Having a serious discussion or argument while driving is dangerous and can increase tension.

2. A woman is thinking about her husband's death

Setting A: A dark, rainy night, alone in her kitchen

Weather affects mood and these conditions will accentuate her sadness and loneliness. A kitchen evokes family meals and happier times, providing a contrast that only increases the heartbreak.

Setting B: Christmas morning, in the living room with her young children

Christmas is generally a happy time, but it will only serve to remind her of what she's lost. She will want to keep it together for the sake of the children, which just adds to the pressure. Gifts that were purchased by or for the husband, memory-rich tree ornaments, an empty place at the table—there will be many reminders of her loss.

Answer Key — Exercise: 10-2

How Setting Affects Stories, continued

Setting C: A lunch with her friend in a fancy restaurant

She will try to maintain her composure in this public setting, but it may not be easy. However, this setting could also work for a not-so-grieving widow, a previously battered or neglected wife, or even a murderer. She will have to keep up appearances, unless her friend is a very close one who knows her secrets.

3. A man pitches an idea for a new product

Setting A: A formal boardroom filled with executives

This traditional setting provides opportunities for showing your character's skills (or not) degree of preparation (or not), and level of comfort (or not). Because it's so traditional, an unexpected element here could provide a good surprise.

Setting B: The boss's office

Depending on the boss, this could be more or less pressure than the boardroom setting. Because it's a one-on-one, the relationship between these two characters is key. A past or present romance, good or bad job performance, company issues or malfeasance, could all play into this setting. Consider also the possibility of an eavesdropper or unexpected party bursting in.

Setting C: An elevator

This tight, enclosed, and time-driven setting offers opportunities for tension and fast pacing. The scene will depend on who is in the elevator (Just the boss? Other management? Other workers? Strangers?) and your character will have to work fast (Google "elevator pitch").

Answer Key
Exercise: 10-3

Conveying Setting Indirectly 1

Convey this information without specifically mentioning the weather, location, or time period. Consider using clothing, furnishings, props, actions, dialogue, sounds, thoughts, food/beverages, scents, emotions, plants/flowers, or tactile details.

It's a hot, muggy summer morning in the 1950s. Your character is in the small kitchen of an old farmhouse in a rural area of Alabama. She cares for her elderly mother, who is in another room.

There is no right answer, but here are some things to consider:

1. You will need to research life in rural Alabama in the 1950s to determine what details you can include that will convey the period (appliances, surfaces, fabrics, tableware, clothing, hairstyles, plants, character names, foods, beverages, etc.).

2. Consider how to show heat and humidity (no air conditioning) in ways such as wiping one's face, condensation on a glass, turning on a fan, or dialogue.

3. Think of what manner of speech, word selection, regionalisms, or other language elements you will use for the main character and the elderly lady, if she speaks.

4. Go beyond the visual and identify any sounds, scents, textures, or other sensual elements that could help bring life to this scene.

Answer Key

Exercise: **10-4**

Conveying Setting Indirectly 2

Convey this information without specifically mentioning the weather, location, or time period. Consider using clothing, furnishings, props, actions, dialogue, sounds, thoughts, food/beverages, scents, emotions, plants/flowers, or tactile details.

A veterinarian has just arrived at her clinic in Seattle. The waiting room is packed with clients and their animals, most of whom are not happy to be there. Several people are in line at the desk, but nobody is behind the counter.

There is no right answer, but here are some things to consider:

1. **You will need to research Seattle to determine the likely weather, architecture, parking situation, and culture (did someone say coffee?).**

2. **Consider how to convey the chaos of the waiting room. Options include animal sounds and scents, people complaining, sounds from back rooms, and phones ringing.**

3. **Think of how your character would react and consider including some information in her dialogue ("Walt! Why isn't anyone at the front desk?").**

4. **An irate customer may also be able to provide insight ("Who cares about free biscotti and organic dog biscuits when we have to sit for an hour to be seen?").**

Answer Key

Exercise: **11-1**

Characters True/False

FALSE The viewpoint character should be like a reporter—conveying all the facts. **The viewpoint character should be key to the story and more than a reporter.**

FALSE Secondary characters should be described at length when they are first introduced. **Secondary character backstories can be woven in later.**

TRUE Each character should have his or her own world with friends, family, problems, opportunities, and desires. **Even if never spelled out to the reader.**

TRUE Every character should figure into the plot and affect the dynamics of other character interactions or create an action that alters the course of the story. **Otherwise the character shouldn't be part of the story.**

TRUE A character should change over time and through experience, based on the events, surroundings, and other characters. **Character development provides interest.**

FALSE Each character should serve a single function, for example comic relief or foil for the main character. **Characters can serve more than one role.**

TRUE Character names that begin with the same letter, rhyme, or sound similar may confuse readers. **Keep readers focused on the story.**

TRUE A character tag tells the reader something about the character. **Even if it's just a quirk.**

FALSE Characters readers recognize, like the shy librarian and the macho handyman, make great secondary characters. **They are stereotypes best avoided.**

FALSE Giving your main character a strong negative trait like racism or cruelty to animals will make the character more believable and appealing to the reader. **Traits that are too negative may turn off readers.**

FALSE The best way to introduce a character is to describe the character's appearance and major traits right away. **Weave descriptions into the story subtly.**

TRUE Dialogue can be a way to convey a character trait. **Dialogue can be revealing.**

FALSE You should give flaws to all characters except the viewpoint character. **No reason to exclude.**

TRUE If you have too many characters, you may be able to have one character serve two purposes. **A common practice.**

TRUE Some character flaws can be endearing and make a character more likeable. **As in life.**

Answer Key — Exercise: 11-2

Bringing Characters to Life (example: TV character Adrian Monk)

1. Provide details or quirks that show individuality.
   Obsessive cleanliness, aversion to germs/touching

2. Show the environment that surrounds the character, particularly the surroundings the character has chosen for himself or herself.
   Home is highly organized and obsessively clean.

3. Have your character fight for something important to him or her.
   Monk mourns his murdered wife and relentlessly tries to find her killer.

4. Give your character a negative trait or flaw that makes the character real without turning off readers.
   Obssessive-compulsiveness

5. Let the character show us who he or she is through unspoken dialogue.
   Monk occasionally "sees" his dead wife and talks to her.

6. Put the character into action—show us what the character does and how, from small mannerisms to heroic (or evil) actions.
   As a detective, Monk's obsessive attention to detail is useful.

7. Show how the character reacts to other people.
   Avoids touching; uses sanitizing wipes after shaking hands.

8. Have something unexpected happen to the character to show how he or she reacts.
   Monk has a persistent nosebleed and must go to the hospital.

9. Show how other people react to the character.
   People find him odd and often underestimate him.

10. Let the character talk and thereby show us who he or she is with dialogue, manner of speech, vocabulary, and expressions.
    Monk has several odd mannerisms and often expresses worries.

11. Show how the character analyzes information, forms strategies, and solves a problem.
    Monk is meticulous, analytical, and notices the tiniest details.

Answer Key

Exercise: 11-3

Conveying Character 1

Using methods other than pure description, write a short piece that conveys some traits of a friend, work colleague, or family member.

> How do you recognize this person? Think not only about the style of their clothes, the color of their hair, and the kind of car they drive, but also about how they put their coat on, how they touch or fidget with their hair, and how they treat others. How do you recognize the person with your eyes shut? Think about speech habits, vocal quirks, frequently used expressions, and how they sneeze or cough. Are they confident or shy? Talkative or quiet? When they greet people do they shake hands, hug, or just smile and say hello? How are their table manners? Do they have an unusual way of eating or distinctive food preferences? When they drive do they yell at other drivers, sing along with the radio, talk to you, or stay silent? A person is much, much more than their physical appearance. Make sure your characters are as well.

Answer Key — Exercise: 11-4

Conveying Character 2

Give the reader a sense of this character through dialogue, action, his thoughts, other character's reactions, etc. Avoid simply describing him with adjectives.

The character is a mature, slim, well-educated man who is quite fond of expensive clothes, shoes, and watches. As he gets ready for the Chamber of Commerce mixer at a local sports bar, he worries that he is overdressed, although he'd prefer that to being underdressed. He isn't fond of mingling, but he hopes to attract clients for his law practice. As he walks into the bar, he learns that to get people to mingle, the host is taping the name of one of the local businesses to each person's back. The attendees are supposed to ask each other questions to find out what business each of them has been given.

There is no one answer, but you could show him getting dressed, naming specific high-end brands of clothing, shoes, and watches. His worries could be expressed through unspoken thoughts or signs of nervousness (fidgeting, putting on and taking off different items). His entering the bar could be shown in a scene with the host and one or more other characters. How he reacts to an embarrassing game would be telling, as would whether he shares these feelings and who he shares them with.

Answer Key
Exercise: 12-1

Point of View True/False

TRUE Point of view affects the way the story is told. **Who tells the story is key.**

FALSE Third-person point of view provides intimacy. **First person provides intimacy.**

TRUE The viewpoint character is the character you use to tell the story. **By definition.**

FALSE The most common point of view used in short stories is second person. **It's rare.**

FALSE Readers like stories in which the point of view shifts among several characters within a scene. **It can be confusing.**

TRUE With a story told in first person, you cannot know what another character is thinking. **Just as in life, you don't know what someone's thinking unless they tell you.**

TRUE In limited third-person point of view, the narrator sees everything but only knows the thoughts of one character. **Similar to, but not as limiting as, first person.**

TRUE A writer must choose the point of view carefully because it affects the facts the reader is privy to. **It can even change the story itself.**

FALSE The viewpoint character should never be the main character. **It's quite common.**

TRUE A first-person narrator must be present in every scene depicted. **I can't know what happens outside my presence unless someone tells me.**

TRUE If you switch to another viewpoint character to tell the same story, the account will likely change. **Just as two people's accounts of something they witness differ.**

FALSE With omniscient third-person point of view you cannot know the thoughts of more than one character. **You can know the thoughts of all the characters.**

Answer Key

Exercise: 12-2

Points of View

Connect the point of view to its characteristics:

First person — This point of view is ideal for intimate or emotional stories, ones with strong main characters, and memoirs.

Second person — This point of view provides an edgier feel, with a narrator that speaks directly to the reader.

Third person — This point of view allows you (with care) to provide insights from multiple characters and offers a bird's-eye view.

Answer Key

Exercise: 12-3

Choosing a Point of View

Choose a point of view (or try several) for telling this story and write it from that perspective.

Erin suspects that her husband, Luke, is cheating on her with someone they socialize with. She and Luke are at a cocktail party when the other woman and her husband arrive and join them. Erin has had too much to drink and keeps making suggestive remarks about the woman. The woman's husband is baffled. Luke just wants to get Erin to go home without making a scene.

Options:

1. **First person from Erin's point of view:** You can provide Erin's thoughts and emotions. She has had too much to drink, so her perceptions may be incorrect, and her feelings may be exaggerated. This will allow the reader to experience her anger and jealousy.

2. **First person from Luke's point of view:** Luke may be angry, embarrassed, ashamed, or worried about the husband's reaction if he realizes what's been going on. You will not be privy to Erin's thoughts or motivations and only able to guess what they are and react to them.

3. **First person from the other woman's point of view:** She may be angry, embarrassed, ashamed or worried about both her husband's reaction and Erin's. She will not know what anyone else is thinking and will have to react to their actions.

4. **Second person:** This will put the reader into the scene as one of the characters ("you"). It's a difficult point of view to sustain and can sometimes be distracting for the reader.

5. **Third person limited (Erin's point of view):** You will be able to provide a larger picture of events while still accessing Erin's (and only Erin's) thoughts. The trade-off will be some loss of intimacy.

6. **Third person omniscient:** You will be describing the scene like a bystander, which will provide an unbiased and unemotional account, but one without any insights.

Answer Key

Exercise: 12-4

Finding Point-of-View Errors

Identify the following point of view errors:

When I smiled, I revealed a piece of spinach in my teeth.
> **In first-person point of view, you cannot see your own face.**

She laughed to herself as Jake handed her a suitcase he had meticulously packed the day before.
> **When you are in one character's head you cannot know what another character has done outside your presence.**

Cameron watched me and thought about how close we had once been.
> **When you're in one person's head you cannot know another person's thoughts.**

I looked out the window but didn't see the cat run by.
> **In first person you can only know what you have seen for yourself.**

Bob came up behind me.
> **Unless you hear him coming, you have no way to know this.**

My face turned red.
> **You cannot see your own face. Substitute "I felt my face flush" or something similar.**

Lakeisha thought about her daughter before answering me.
> **You cannot know what Lakeisha is thinking unless she tells you.**

I caught his eye and he turned.
> **You don't know why he turned. A substitute could be "He turned and saw me." or something similar.**

Rachel came in after I went to sleep and pulled my blanket up.
> **You cannot know something that happens when you are asleep. You can find the blanket has been pulled up and suspect Rachel has come in.**

Answer Key

Exercise: **12-4**

Finding Point-of-View Errors, continued

Ted opened the letter and was shocked by what he read.
> **You can't know Ted's reaction unless you see it. Mention a shocked look.**

She recalled this happening before as she handed me the phone.
> **You don't know what she recalled unless she tells you.**

Jamal walked in but didn't notice I had turned the lights down.
> **You don't know what he did or didn't notice. You can say that he didn't seem to notice.**

"What did you say?" I asked, my eyes dilating with anger.
> **You can't see your own eyes. Use a different action to indicate anger.**

Answer Key — Exercise: 13-1

Dialogue True/False

TRUE Dialogue can reveal character traits. **What a character says can be illuminating.**

FALSE Dialogue should be more formal than the way people really speak. **It should be the same.**

TRUE A dialogue tag is the "he said" or "she said" that follows characters speaking. **The tag can be any vocalization (he whispered, she yelled).**

FALSE Never use contractions (we'll, let's, I'd) in dialogue. **They are a part of natural speech.**

TRUE In dialogue, it's OK to have grammatical errors. **If it fits the character.**

TRUE Dialogue is a good way to convey character. **It can tell readers a great deal.**

TRUE It's acceptable to use made-up words like "ginormous" and nonstandard words like "ain't" in dialogue. **If it fits the character.**

FALSE Setting cannot be conveyed through dialogue. **Dialogue can provide clues to setting.**

TRUE Unspoken thoughts, inner dialogue, internal monologue, and unspoken dialogue all mean the same thing. **They all are thoughts that are conveyed to the reader but not spoken.**

TRUE A good way to check dialogue authenticity is to read it aloud. **It can be helpful.**

FALSE When "said" has been used already, find a synonym like "mentioned" to use in its place. **"Said" blends in; overly complicated tags can be distracting.**

TRUE Dialogue can reveal conflict. **Dialogue is a great way to show conflict.**

TRUE Dialogue combined with action can add impact and control pace. **Very effective.**

TRUE Characters' spoken and unspoken dialogue should be consistent with their backgrounds, education, culture, and other factors. **Otherwise the characters don't ring true.**

FALSE Long pieces of dialogue are a great way to provide backstory. **Boring and unrealistic.**

TRUE Dialogue tags must be vocalizations. **You can't laugh, sigh, or cough words.**

FALSE Characters should never interrupt each other in dialogue. **It's common in life.**

Answer Key

Exercise: **13-2**

Correcting Dialogue Errors

What are some things you might change about this exchange?

"How are you today?" Mary asked.

Although this is realistic in the sense that it's something people often say, it doesn't provide any insights about the setting, characters, or situation.

"Fine," said John.

Again, this is something people say all the time. You could show irritation by having John immediately turn his back or some other action to indicate that he is actually not fine.

"I saw your sister, Helen, who is a teacher," said Mary.

You may want to get this information to the reader, but in real conversations, people don't tell people things they already know. Even providing the name "Helen," unless there is more than one sister, will seem odd to the reader.

"That's a surprise," John said in astonishment.

The dialogue tag is redundant (we already know it's a surprise). If you want to take it up a notch, add an action or change the quoted section to something less explanatory ("Wow" or a curse, for example).

"She said to give you this book about bats, which is old and moldy but looks expensive. I think it must be very valuable," she exclaimed.

Telling rather than showing, combined with redundancy. It is also not an exclamation, so the dialogue tag is incorrect, and the use of "she" to indicate two different people within one paragraph is confusing. You could convey old and moldy by having her blow dust off, sneeze, or mention an odor.

Answer Key

Exercise: **13-2**

Correcting Dialogue Errors, continued

"That's what you think," he laughed.
> **You can't laugh words, so the dialogue tag is incorrect.**

"I hate loud restaurants." *If there's anything I can't stand it's loud restaurants.*
> **Unspoken dialogue should provide insight, not just repeat dialogue that is spoken.**

"I'm here for you," said Colin.

"I know," said Jen.

"No matter what," said Colin.

"It's just that Holly—" said Jen.

"Never mind Holly," said Colin.

> **If it's been established that only two people are talking in a back and forth manner, it is not necessary to keep repeating the dialogue tags:**
>
> **"I'm here for you," said Colin.**
>
> **"I know," said Jen.**
>
> **"No matter what."**
>
> **"It's just that Holly—"**
>
> **"Never mind Holly."**

Answer Key

Exercise: 13-3

Enhancing Dialogue with Action

Experiment with adding different actions to change the meaning of this piece of dialogue.

"I do love you, Doug said _____.

Here are some options, but there are many:

"I do love you," Doug said, as he got down on one knee.

"I do love you," Doug said, stifling a yawn.

"I do love you," Doug said, dabbing his eyes with a tissue.

"I do love you," Doug said, taking her hand.

"I do love you," Doug said, wiping his nose on his sleeve.

"I do love you," Doug said, adding *when you're not being a bitch* in his mind.

Answer Key Exercise: 13-4

Unspoken Dialogue

Which of the following would be good opportunities for unspoken dialogue?

1. A man recalling what he had for breakfast
2. (A woman lying to her husband) ✓
3. (A man thinking about his former wife while talking to his current one) ✓
4. A forgetful woman remembering she needs a dental appointment
5. (Showing a character's fear of heights) ✓
6. Providing information about something that happened to another character
7. (Conveying a character's hopes for her child) ✓
8. (Showing a character saying something but meaning something different) ✓
9. Conveying a character's backstory
10. Showing a character's expert knowledge about termites
11. Conveying the thoughts of a non-viewpoint character

Answer Key

Exercise: **14-1**

The Title True/False

FALSE The title should explain what the story is about. **Don't give too much away.**

TRUE An obscure term from the story could be used in a title. **Could be intriguing.**

TRUE The title should be in keeping with the style and content of the story. **Don't mislead.**

FALSE A title should never be fewer than three words or longer than six. **Could be either.**

TRUE The title is an opportunity for the writer to talk directly to the reader. **Absolutely.**

TRUE It's a good idea to have a working title when you start writing. **Reevaluate later.**

FALSE A title should be as short as possible. **Not necessarily.**

FALSE The title should provide the theme for the story. **Not necessarily.**

FALSE You should choose a title before starting to write so you don't get off track. **No reason to pen yourself in.**

TRUE Your title shouldn't give away too much. **Make it intriguing, not obvious.**

FALSE A foreign term should not be used in a title. **It could provoke curiosity.**

TRUE A phrase from a poem might be used as a title. **A legitimate option.**

FALSE The moral of the story should be its title. **Too obvious.**

FALSE A line of dialogue should never be used as a title. **That might work well.**

TRUE An ending might pay off the title by giving the reader the information necessary to understand its meaning. **Could make for a satisfying conclusion.**

FALSE A title should never be ambiguous. **Ambiguity creates curiosity.**

Answer Key Exercise: 14-2

Choosing a Title 1

What are some possible titles for this story?

You know you shouldn't accept a third Tanqueray & tonic, but you're enjoying the attentions of this beachy lifeguard. Andy. Even his name is cute. So what if he's at least ten years younger than you—all the better that he doesn't seem to notice. You revel in feeling like a college girl, even though you're long past your sorority days. This is what you had hoped would happen on this weekend at the beach—this time away from the job hunt, the family responsibilities, and the monotony of monogamy, a.k.a. your marriage to Jack.

You only half-wish that Fran had stayed at The Starboard with you. Sure, this weekend wasn't so great so far, but this was supposed to be a reunion. Has it really been fourteen years since you and she were roommates at American University? You can't believe that time has rushed through your life as fast as your son Max used to tear down the hallway to escape a bath when he was a toddler. But fourteen years? You do the math. Max was born the winter after graduation, and he just turned thirteen in April. My God! Sometimes you forget, or at least try to forget, that you're the mother of a teenager.

You wish you hadn't thought of Max just now. What would your son think if he knew that Mom was weighing her morals vs. her needs? And at this moment, your needs are the larger of the two. You and Jack are "having problems," as the cliché goes. Jack's been distant, and you've been distant, and maybe the distance this weekend might be the cure. Or maybe not. At the very least, this weekend in Dewey will be a litmus test.

There are no right answers, but the title Nancy Sherman chose was "A Cougar at The Starboard." You might use phrases from the story (litmus test, the cure, or weekend in Dewey), play off the themes of reunion and second chances, or pull out a specific detail (Tanqueray & tonic, The Starboard).

Answer Key

Exercise: **14-3**

Choosing a Title 2

Your story features a Civil War soldier who is writing a letter to his girlfriend the day before a big battle. Check the best options for the title:

√ A Civil War-era term that could have double meaning

An excellent choice that telegraphs the setting and yet provides some intrigue.

A phrase that lets readers know the soldier didn't survive

Not a good option as it gives too much away.

"Letter from a Soldier"

Possible, but a bit too literal and not terribly interesting.

√ A phrase from the letter

May be a good option if it gives the reader a sense of the story

Reference to a concept such as hope, fear, or courage

Possible, but such a common theme that it probably won't set the story apart from many others and gives no sense of this specific story.

√ An ambiguous romantic phrase

Another possible choice that would set the tone without giving too much away.

Answer Key — Exercise: 15-1

Editing True/False

TRUE The three main types of editing are: developmental editing, copy editing, and proofreading. **Manuscripts generally need all three.**

FALSE Copy editing includes recommending scene rearrangement or other structural changes. **That's developmental editing.**

TRUE Style guides go beyond grammar rules to include recommendations for consistent formatting, capitalization, and abbreviations. **They are the copy editor's reference.**

FALSE Copy editors also do developmental editing. **Not usually. Developmental editing requires different skills.**

TRUE A good way to check story structure is to cut it into scenes and move them around. **It can be a useful exercise.**

FALSE Developmental editing involves correcting grammar, spelling, and punctuation. **That is copy editing.**

FALSE Automatic spellcheckers and grammar programs are always correct. **Not so!**

TRUE During editing you should check for commonly confused words such as peek, peak, and pique. **These are easy mistakes to make and even easier to miss.**

FALSE Proofreading is the first step in editing. **It is the last step.**

TRUE Most writers have a writing tic—a word, phrase, or punctuation mark they use too much. **Common ones are overuse of exclamation points and dashes.**

TRUE A good way to check rhythm and pacing is to read the manuscript out loud. **A good practice.**

TRUE Proofreading includes checking for inadvertently omitted words. **These errors are hard to catch.**

FALSE Most manuscripts just need proofreading. **Most need all three kinds of editing.**

TRUE Grammar, spelling, and punctuation mistakes can pull the reader out of your fictional world. **Any mistake can break the spell.**

Answer Key

Exercise: 15-2

Types of Editing

Which type of editing deals with each of these items? Write "DE" for developmental editing, "CE" for copy editing, or "PR" for proofreading.

- **PR** Incorrect type size
- **DE** Poor ending
- **PR** Page heading incorrect
- **DE** Point-of-view error
- **CE** Removing incorrect apostrophe in "it's"
- **CE** Redundant word or phrase
- **DE** Time-inappropriate character
- **CE** Incorrect dialogue tag
- **DE** Need for more conflict or another setback
- **CE** Spelling error
- **CE** Character name wrong in two places
- **DE** Changing where story starts
- **CE** Incorrect spelling of "their" as "they're"
- **CE** Incorrect italics
- **PR** Wrong page number
- **CE** Clichéd or overused phrase
- **DE** Scene out of order
- **DE** Inside wrong character's head for point of view

Answer Key

Exercise: **15-3**

Identifying Writing Errors

Identify the problem with each of these sentences:

1. He woke up sick as a dog.

   Cliché. Choose a better way to convey his condition.

2. Damn! It was her turn! He was sick of it! He vowed to get revenge!

   Overuse of exclamation marks. Save them for real exclamations (like "Damn!").

3. The train stopped at the station in Albany. She was unfamiliar with it.

   Is she unfamiliar with the train, the station, or Albany? "It" has no clear reference.

4. "That's my coat," she laughed.

   You can't laugh words, so this is an incorrect dialogue tag.

5. The carpenter looked at the various sizes of nails and chose the he thought would work best.

   The word "one" has been omitted (chose the *one* he thought…).

6. "It's a really big house," he said loudly.

   This would be better written as: "It's a mansion," he yelled.

7. Cindy stood up and blinked her eyes. She put her PIN number into the ATM machine that was in close proximity to her house. The bank had offered a free gift for new customers.

   Redundancies: stood up, blinked her eyes, PIN number, ATM machine, close proximity, and free gift.

8. Marsha put her paper dolls away. It was time to go to see *Frozen 2* with her parents.

   Time-inappropriate character—her name and playing with paper dolls is suitable for a child in the 1950s, not the 2020s.

9. "Their's nothing in here," he said, peaking into the box.

   Spelling—"their's" instead of "there's" and "peaking" instead of "peeking."

Answer Key
Exercise: 15-3

Identifying Writing Errors, continued

10. "I'll get right on that," said three-year-old Carol. "It's right in my wheelhouse."

    Age-inappropriate dialogue—this does not sound like a three-year-old. Age-inappropriate name—Carol is an unlikely name for a contemporary child.

11. He walked slowly.

    Choose a stronger verb rather than relying on an adverb: He strolled (or ambled or meandered).

12. "Where is it?" he bellowed. "It's behind you," she explained. "Thanks," he acknowledged. "You're welcome," she conceded.

    Distracting dialogue tags—stick to "said," "asked," and "replied," when possible. Once it's established that there are only two people, no tags are needed.

13. The clock chimed as I slept.

    The speaker can't know what went on while she was asleep.

14. *I thought about it and decided to pick her up later.*

    Incorrect use of italics. This is not an actual thought; the speaker is describing a thought.

15. They consider chocolate a health food because its full of antioxidants.

    Missing apostrophe in "its": it's.

16. The movie was better than anyone in audience had expected.

    Missing word—"the" (anyone in *the* audience...).

17. "I hope your feeling better."

    Incorrect spelling—"your" should be "you're."

18. His favorite television show was was "The Masked Singer."

    Repeated word—"was."

Answer Key

Exercise: **15-4**

Redundancy

Identify what is wrong with the following excerpts:

1. "It's you!" she said. "I'm so excited to see you! You've always been my best friend!

    Overuse of exclamation marks and redundant content.

2. 8 a.m. in the morning

    "In the morning" is unnecessary—"a.m." means the same thing.

3. It was snowing. White flakes fell from the sky.

    The second sentence contains the same information as the first.

4. It was red in color.

    Red is already a color; there's nothing else it can be.

5. The ring was really unique.

    "Unique" is an absolute (like "dead"); either it's unique (one of a kind) or it isn't.

6. It was an unexpected surprise.

    If it was a surprise, it was unexpected.

7. We had no advance warning.

    A warning is providing cautionary information in advance.

8. She had gotten big as a house.

    "As a house" is cliché and doesn't add information.

9. When it first began.

    "First" doesn't add anything.

10. She learned she had the HIV virus.

    The "V" in "HIV" stands for virus, so this says "the human immunodeficiency virus virus."

11. That's a small speck of dirt.

    "Speck" means small.

12. Be there at twelve noon.

    "Twelve" is redundant. Noon *is* twelve.

13. That was the end result.

    The result is the end.

215

Answer Key

Exercise: **16-1**

Facts, Logic, and Lawyers True/False

FALSE Fact-checking is not required if the story is fiction. **It's just as important.**

FALSE Quoting song lyrics is fine as long as you cite the songwriter's name. **Definitely not.**

TRUE Writers should take great care when using real people as models for characters. **Unless you enjoy lawsuits.**

FALSE Material on the internet is not copyrighted so it can be used. **Not true.**

TRUE With fantasy or science fiction, you are free to create any reality you want, as long as the rules are consistent. **It's called *world building*.**

FALSE Using several paragraphs of a poem would probably be considered fair use, as long as you don't quote the entire poem. **Likely a copyright violation.**

FALSE It's usually not necessary to check details on a story that takes place in current time and a well-known place. **Readers will notice if you make a mistake.**

FALSE Real people can be used as characters in a book if their names are changed. **No they can't.**

FALSE Because restaurants are open to the public, a fictional story about someone getting food poisoning at a real restaurant would be acceptable. **Another possible lawsuit.**

TRUE Quoting a single sentence from a novel (and giving credit) would probably be considered fair use. **That would likely be OK.**

TRUE Trademarked brand names are legally protected, but they can be used if they are capitalized and not shown in a negative way. **But be careful.**

TRUE When using a flash forward, you should check the timeline to make sure character ages and other facts are correct. **Mistakes draw readers out of the story.**

FALSE It would be OK to publish an old diary you bought at a thrift store. **You own a copy, not the copyright.**

TRUE A factual error can pull the reader out of the story. **The spell is broken.**

TRUE Individuals have a right to privacy that extends to not being written about without their permission. **Especially true of people not in the public arena.**

Answer Key
Exercise: 16-2

Checking the Facts

Circle things in the following paragraph that should be verified.

> (Marlene) Williams ate her (raisin bran) before asking her mother if she could go to a friend's house after school. Her friend lived on Oak Street, (only a few) blocks away from (Gramwood Elementary School) in (Memphis). It was warm for February and they'd be getting a long weekend for Martin Luther King Day. She gazed out the window, past the (camelia blossoms), to the condo building across (the street). A (city bus) had just pulled up (in front of) the building and an (elderly man) was getting out.

Is "Marlene" a plausible first name for a school-age character in current time? Check the Social Security database to confirm.

Is "raisin bran" a trademark? If so, it should be capitalized.

Is Gramwood Elementary School an actual school in Memphis? If so, verify spelling

Is Oak Street within a few blocks of the school?

Does Martin Luther King Day ever occur in February? Is it observed by school closures in Memphis?

Are there camelias in Memphis and, if so, would they be blooming in February?

Are there any condo buildings on streets adjacent to Oak Street?

Are there city buses in Memphis and, if so, do they operate on the street where the condo is located?

Does the city bus pull up to the front of the condo building and, if so, would a person emerging be visible from a house on Oak Street?

Answer Key — Exercise: 16-3

Fact-Checking Resources

Match the fact with a reputable source for verification:

How to spell a word
Dictionary

Whether a building has a thirteenth floor
Visit or interview with reputable local source

Whether the first name for a character born in 1910 is plausible
Social Security Administration website

Whether to capitalize "army"
Style guide such as *The Chicago Manual of Style*

How many people live in a city
Almanac (www.almanac.com)

When the word "menthol" came into use
Dictionary

Whether a house built in 1890 still exists
Visit or interview with reputable local source

The mission of a charitable organization
Website or printed material provided by the organization

The proper spelling of a brand name
Website or printed material provided by the company

Whether there are cases of tuberculosis in the United States
Government (.gov) website

What time the sun set on a day in 1983
Almanac (www.almanac.com)

Note that Wikipedia is not considered a reputable source for fact-checking.

Answer Key — Exercise: 17-1

Marketing Short Stories True/False

FALSE Take care where you submit because short stories can only be sold once. **Not if you've kept the rights to your story (which you should).**

TRUE Contests can be a good way for a writer to practice the submission process. **Definitely.**

TRUE If your goal is publication, it's a good idea to research potential markets before you even begin writing. **Otherwise you may be wasting your time.**

TRUE Magazines and journals generally specify the length of short stories they accept. **If you don't see guidelines on their website, request them.**

FALSE Writer's guidelines are helpful, but you shouldn't treat them as rules. **Yes you should.**

FALSE When submitting to a special-interest magazine (such as *Woman's Day*), you can improve your chances by submitting a story outside that interest. **You'll waste time and effort.**

TRUE Knowing the audience of the publication you're submitting to can be helpful. **Absolutely.**

TRUE If your story deals with a topic or interest (knitting, for instance), publications devoted to that subject may be good submission opportunities. **Target your submissions.**

TRUE A contest prize of editing services may be a red flag that the company is trying to sell its services rather than run a legitimate contest. **Be wary.**

FALSE When you submit to a publisher, it helps to have a cute email address such as iloveunicorns@gmail.com. **Unprofessional submissions hurt your odds.**

FALSE Most publishers don't care if submissions have grammar and spelling errors because they have editors who can fix them. **You look bad and will make more work for them.**

TRUE Writing to a niche means choosing a specific category such as sailing or older-adult romance and writing a story that fits to increase the odds of acceptance. **An effective approach.**

FALSE When you submit your story, it's a good idea to have a cover letter in which you say that, although you don't like to read and hate short stories, you've always wanted to be published and your kids think your story is really great. **Not impressive.**

FALSE The more expensive it is to enter a contest, the more likely it is that the contest is legitimate. **The opposite is often the case.**

FALSE If a magazine only accepts flash fiction, you can submit a 5,000-word short story if it's really good because the magazine's editor could probably cut it down to the proper length. **You can but you'll waste everyone's time.**

FALSE If the writer's guidelines specify submissions by mail, it's still a good idea to send a few emails or make calls to see whether they've made a decision yet. **A good way to annoy an editor.**

Answer Key

Exercise: 17-2

Why Would You Want to Enter a Contest?

Check the reasons you might choose to enter a writing contest.

√ To gain a publishing credential

If the prize includes publication, this could be a good reason to enter.

To earn enough money to retire

That's probably not going to happen.

√ To help sell books you've written

A great reason if winning the contest provides exposure for your other work.

To get in an anthology that isn't very good, but at least your work will get published

Do you really want to be published that badly?

√ To help get other things you've written published

It could happen. Contest wins look great on an author bio or submission.

To get your writing on the internet

Beware. You may not be able market the work to other outlets once it's appeared online.

√ To gain exposure for your writing

Yes! Publicity can be great for a writer.

To pay off your student debt

Dream on.

√ To get experience writing to a word count, editing, and submitting

A great reason for a new/beginning writer to try a contest.

To win a discount for a book coach

Danger! This kind of prize is a red flag for a bogus contest.

To get a lot of work out there so chances of success are increased

Focus on quality, not quantity.

Answer Key — Exercise: 17-3

Contest Red Flags

Circle the signs that might be cause for concern.

1. ⟨The contest is run by a literary agency, and the prize is representation.⟩
2. There is no entry fee. **Not a red flag on its own.**
3. The contest has multiple categories for novels but none for short stories.
4. The entry fee is low.
5. The contest is open only to students.
6. ⟨The prize money depends on the number of entries.⟩
7. ⟨The entry fee is excessively high.⟩
8. ⟨The contest has twenty categories for short stories.⟩
9. ⟨You notice that the same contest is being run under different names.⟩
10. The contest is run by a company you've never heard of. **Not a red flag on its own.**
11. ⟨A friend entered the contest last year and now gets lots of emails promoting publishing services and products.⟩
12. ⟨You get repeated unsolicited email promotions for the contest.⟩
13. ⟨The prize is a credit toward or discount on products or services.⟩
14. ⟨The registration form requires you to agree to publication without compensation.⟩
15. ⟨A company runs multiple contests simultaneously or a contest every month.⟩
16. ⟨The award is a trophy or plaque that you must pay for.⟩
17. ⟨You can't find any guidelines or criteria for judging.⟩
18. The contest is run by a publishing company.

Answer Key
Exercise: 17-3

Contest Red Flags, continued

19. ~~The company seems focused more on soliciting entries than on the awards themselves.~~

20. ~~The contest's deadline is a year or more out or gets postponed with no winners announced.~~

21. ~~Winners are required to buy copies of the anthology.~~

22. The contest is being run for the first time.

23. ~~There is no apparent human involvement (generic email address, online payment, no contact information on website or no website, emails with questions go unanswered).~~

24. ~~You must sign a contract assigning all rights to the publisher.~~

25. ~~If you win, there will be additional costs (critiques, editing, agency fees, etc.).~~

26. ~~The registration form asks for information such as social security number, mother's maiden name, or scan of driver's license or passport as proof of identity.~~

27. The prize is publication.

28. The contest is limited to writers in a certain region, of a certain age, or with a specific ethnicity.

29. ~~The prize is publicity or a marketing package.~~

30. ~~The sponsor reserves the right to substitute prizes, delay prizes for insufficient entries, or reduce prizes if certain conditions aren't met.~~

31. ~~The terms and conditions are vague or confusing.~~

Answer Key

Exercise: **17-4**

Understanding Guidelines

Read the guidelines below and then answer the questions that follow.

Tempting magazine is seeking submissions of short fiction (300-2,000 words) that deal with temptations (food, drink, shopping, activities). Our audience is women and men (3-1 women to men), aged 34-65. We do not accept sexually explicit material or stories that shame or preach. We are in need of stories from all parts of the United States, particularly out-of-the-way areas. Submit manuscripts using the link below. No simultaneous submissions, please. We buy first rights only.

1. Should you submit a poem to this magazine?

    No. They are looking for short fiction.

2. Should you submit a 1,500-word article about how the brain reacts to temptation?

    No. They are seeking fiction, not nonfiction.

3. Should you email your submission?

    No. They have requested online submissions through a link on the website.

4. To stand out, would it be good to send a 250-word story?

    No. The minimum word count is 300 words.

5. Should you submit a racy romance?

    No. They do not accept sexually explicit material.

6. Should you submit a story about two millennials who meet on a gaming site?

    No. This story would be better suited to a magazine focused on that age range.

7. Should you submit a story for children about the temptation of candy?

    No. This story would be better suited to a publication for children.

8. To stand out, would it be good to send a story that takes place in Alaska?

    Yes. They are specifically seeking stories from out-of-the-way places, so a story outside the continental United States might attract their attention.

Answer Key

Exercise: **17-4**

Understanding Guidelines, continued

9. Should you submit a story about a woman who loves smoking and how she deals with lung cancer?

    No. Although this publication would probably take a story about smoking, it does not want stories that shame or preach.

10. Should you send a story about a man who loves cigars who meets a woman who loves cigars?

    Yes. This story fits their demographics and stated needs.

11. Should you submit a 1,700-word story about a cat that loves to swim in the ocean?

    No. While the word count is within the limit, the subject matter is outside their interests.

12. Should you submit a story about an eighty-year-old woman?

    Probably not. Unless it's an unusual spin, the readers are younger and most publications prefer stories about people of the same age as their readers.

13. Should you submit a story about the bistros of Paris?

    No. This publication wants stories that take place in the United States.

14. Should you submit a story you sent to another publication, since you haven't heard from them?

    Not unless you withdraw it from consideration by the other publication. This publication does not accept simultaneous submissions.

15. Should you submit a story about women who own wineries in the United States?

    Yes. This sounds like a good fit.

16. Should you submit a story that has already been published in another magazine?

    No. This publication buys first rights only, so you should only submit stories that have not been previously published.

17. To stand out, would it be good to send a 320-word story about a company that ships oysters from an island in Maryland?

    Yes. A story on the short side of the desired word count that fits the other criteria may have a better chance of acceptance as it would be easier to fit into the available space.

Answer Key — Exercise: 18-1

Match Terms with Definitions

Match each word or phrase with its definition:

Viewpoint character: **Character through which the story is told**

Backstory: **A character's or situation's background and what led up to this point in the story**

Telling detail: **An illuminating detail that provides insight into a character or situation**

Writer's guidelines: **A publisher's rules for accepting a writing submission**

Unspoken thoughts: **What a character is thinking (also called unspoken dialogue or inner dialogue)**

Show, don't tell: **Use action and dialogue instead of narration**

Filter words: **Words that separate the reader from the emotion**

Bookending: **Echoing an object, line of dialogue, situation, or other element from the beginning of the story at the end**

Theme: **The underlying message of the story**

Hook: **An engaging element, often at the start of a story, that captures the reader's interest**

Conflict: **An internal or external pressure on the character that makes the reader care about the story's outcome**

Pace: **The varying speed at which the story moves forward**

Flash forward: **A time skip to a future point, conveyed as a scene, with a return to present time at its conclusion**

Scene: **A situation conveyed in real time that contains characters, setting, conflict, and resolution, and that moves the story forward**

Flashback: **An account of an event that took place in the past, written in present tense, that returns to present time at its conclusion**

Point of view: **The place from which the story is told, usually one of the characters or a narrator**

Copy editor: **Person who corrects mistakes in grammar, spelling, and punctuation**

Spellchecker: **Automatic editor, which may or may not be correct**

Raise the stakes: **Increase the danger, conflict, or importance of a goal**

Answer Key   Exercise: 18-2

Match Terms with Examples

Match each word or phrase with an example:

Genre: **Science fiction**

Dialogue tag: **He said**

Publication outlet: **A literary journal**

Passive voice: **The door was closed by Sally.**

Transition: **Later that same day...**

Premise: **A veteran finds it difficult to deal with his son's interest in online war games.**

Antagonist: **The Joker from the Batman series**

Raise the stakes: **When the negotiator arrived, he learned that his wife was one of the hostages.**

Personality flaw: **A character's inability to empathize with others**

Symbol: **Flower buds opening to signal regeneration**

Answer Key
Exercise: 18-3

The World's Worst Short Story

[Generic title—be more creative]

A Birthday Story

[Factual error—no hills in Forreston, IL]

[Forreston spelled incorrectly]

[Unlikely character name]

Kaylee Hernandez was born in the hills of Foreston, Illinois.

[Dull beginning—backstory]

[Abrupt change in tense]

She had two brothers. She also has a sister. She has brown tresses

[Poor details and redundant]

and brown eyes. Today is her sixteenth birthday. She will be big for

[Changed tense again]

her age. She had a happy childhood. *I am so lucky*, she thought to

[No character insights or reason to be interested]

herself. *I am too*, thought her sister.

[Head hopping]

[Repetitive sentence structure, redundant]

[Telling, not showing—show us the door swinging open, let us hear the bell on the door or feel the rush of cold air from outside]

One day, Kayli went to the store. The brakes were slammed

[Character's name misspelled]

[Passive voice—try: She slammed on the brakes]

on by her when she parked. She got out of the car quickly.

[Stronger verb instead of adverb: She jumped from her car.]

"Are those tomatoes on sale?" she asked quizzically.

[Unnecessary and redundant dialogue tag]

"Yes!" laughed the store manager. "They are Nigerian-grown

[Dialogue tag not a vocalization]

[No description or characterization—we don't even know if it's a man or a woman. Is there a reason he or she is laughing? We don't know.]

227

The World's Worst Short Story, continued

and shipped on dole container ships to Philadelphia, where they are [Capitalize brand names]

off-loaded and transferred to flat-bed trucks." [Info dump]

"I love tomatoes!" exclaimed Kayley ecstatically. [Character's name misspelled] [Redundant dialogue tag]

"Me too," said the store manager. [No need to repeat dialogue tags when it's clear only two people are speaking]

Now that she is eighty, Kayly knows their are more ways to celebrate a birthday then they're used to be! [Large shift in time with no transition] [An 80-year-old Kaylee? Highly unlikely. Name also misspelled again.] ["There," "their," and "they're" are commonly confused. "Then" and "than" are also commonly confused.]

Then she woke up. It had all been a dream! That's when she realized that there's no place like home. [Cliché ending] [Overuse of exclamation points] [Hitting the reader over the head with the theme] [Two spaces in between sentences (there should only be one space)] [Abrupt and poorly-thought-out ending] [No conflict. Without a conflict to resolve, the reader has no stake in the story and no reason to care for the character.]

www.ingramcontent.com/pod-product-compliance
Lightning Source LLC
Chambersburg PA
CBHW081107080526

44587CB00021B/3482